HOMEOWNER'S GUIDE TO LANDSCAPING THAT SAVES ENERGY DOLLARS

HOMEOWNER'S GUIDE TO LANDSCAPING THAT SAVES ENERGY DOLLARS

Ruth S. Foster

Illustrations by James Lombardi

DAVID McKAY COMPANY, INC. • NEW YORK

LIBRARY OF CONGRESS CATALOGING IN PUBLICATION DATA
Foster, Ruth S
    Homeowner's guide to landscaping that saves energy
dollars.
    Includes index.
    1. Landscape gardening. 2. Dwellings—Energy
conservation. I. Title.
SB473.F67   635.9   78-2506
ISBN 0-679-50863-5
ISBN 0-679-50866-X pbk.

10 9 8 7 6 5 4 3 2
MANUFACTURED IN THE UNITED STATES OF AMERICA

CONTENTS

PART

I

THE THEORY

1

ENERGY, CLIMATE, AND HUMAN COMFORT

Environmentalists are accused of wanting us all to freeze in the dark. Oil barons are accused of wanting to suspend us, coughing, in air-conditioned skyscrapers above polluted cities. Somewhere between the two is a rational compromise.

Ever since the first caveman moved indoors and lit a fire in the darkness, man has used his ingenuity and what was at hand to make himself more comfortable. The land around us provides many opportunities for energy saving. If we understand how our environment functions, then we can change it to suit our needs. To change our surroundings in an esthetically pleasing way is called landscaping: the art of sculpturing the land, and what grows on it, to serve us.

Man has long raped the land, unmindful of the consequences. What was the Biblical land of milk and honey is now the desert of the Middle East. Shepherds overgrazed the sod. Most vegetation disappeared. Today, that desert absorbs sunlight during day and is unbearably hot. Because that land has no green canopy to protect it from the black, night sky, then it is cold and windy. Good plants can't get a foothold.

The deserts, however, can be made to bloom again. There are reclamation projects, most sucessful in Israel. Once forests are re-established, the nearby houses become pleasant places during day and cozy at night. A house in the woods is more comfortable than one on the romantic but uncomfortable desert sands.

In the early days of the United States, southwest Indians made use of their desert land for climate control. Their pueblos were built under cliff overhangs, which protected the dwellings from the high sun in summer, yet admitted the lower winter sun. These houses, built into hillsides, had thick walls with small openings to conserve heat at night and preserve coolness during the day. In parts of the Sahara and Turkey, people still live in caves to escape the uncomfortable climate extremes outside. So do modern Australian opal miners.

You may not have a cliff or a cave on your lot, but the same principles still apply.

In cold New England, the early settlers learned how to use the sun. For them, a south-facing window meant less time chopping wood. The barns and outbuildings were usually to the north side of the house, against the wind, but the orchards were protected from it. Indian attackers hid behind trees and shrubs near the house, so such plantings were impractical, though they would have provided additional wind protection. Settlers on the prairies, how-

Montezuma's Castle—Pueblo Dwelling, Arizona

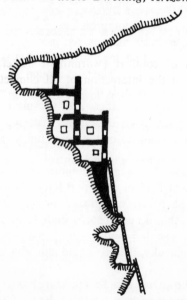

ever, did use trees and shrubs for wind protection. Windbreaks are still a necessary, significant feature of the Midwestern plains.

CLIMATE

Landscaping to save energy dollars involves changing the climate around a building in order to reduce the cost of cooling, heating, and irrigating.

Climate is shaped by many factors including sun, wind, temperature, humidity, solar radiation, evaporation, precipitation, and thermal differentials. These factors are then influenced by land and ocean, wind direction, mountains, cloud patterns, cities, snow, thunderstorm frequency, gravity, and air pressure. All together they add up to our climate.

Climate is a geographic term. Some regional climates affect large areas. Some local climates affect only a town, a valley, or a mountain. Smaller still are microclimates, so limited they affect only one street, one side of a lake, or even one side of a building. The lot on which your house is built (or will be built) has its own microclimate. By adjusting that small part of the atmosphere, you can significantly reduce your energy costs.

The more buildings your area has, the more the regional climate is modified. Also, the more buildings, the more different microclimates will there be. These are also referred to technically as microenvironments.

The sensation of comfort (warmth in winter, coolness in summer) depends on the interaction of all climactic factors. A careful analysis of the local climatic elements identifies those you can use or control.

What are the most unpleasant aspects of your microclimate? What are the most troublesome? What features are most comfortable? The ultimate aim of climate control is to improve human comfort.

To create that sense of comfort, we use energy in furnaces, air conditioners, dehumidifiers, and fans. Cutting down your use of these mechanical appliances saves energy—and dollars. It can be done to a great extent through landscaping. Once trees are growing, they cost hardly anything compared to electricity or fuel oil.

The savings can be significant. For instance, one mature tree provides as much cooling as five 10,000 BTU air conditioners.

If you think that's peanuts, consider Richmond, Virginia. A tree survey estimated that without its 200,000 public shade trees, the city would have to spend $827,793 a day for equivalent air conditioning.

MICROCLIMATES

Microclimates are small areas in which conditions and temperatures vary one from the other. One microclimate, such as a sunny, paved corner between two buildings, may be hot. Another, downwind from a small lake, may be breezy and cool. The lake's upwind side will feel hotter and be drier. The microclimate under a grove of trees is quite different from that along a paved city street. The street will feel up to 25 degrees warmer. (It may be as much as 15 degrees warmer in fact.) In summer, that calls for more air conditioning in adjacent houses. In winter, warm paved streets help to save heating costs. A windy mountain canyon presents yet a different set of characteristics.

Each microclimate around a house requires a certain amount of energy to make the house and yard comfortable. Chances are that your house's microclimate uses excess energy and costs you more money than it should. In cold climates, a hot paved corner will warm that side of the building and extend the comfortable outdoor season. Winds in a canyon can be channeled to cool in summer. (A bonus is that mosquitoes don't like windy spots.)

And each location has certain plants that will grow and thrive. The planting of cactus in a winter garden, or azaleas on the North Dakota plains, requires horticultural gymnastics for decent survival. Matching plant material and microenvironments is more sensible. The best cost-benefit ratios, growth rates, and lowest maintenance always accompany plants that are genetically adapted to their microenvironments.

Before planting, determine the energy potentials of your microclimate and then analyze your area for soil, maintenance, esthetic, and horticultural requirements.

THE COMFORT FACTOR

If energy strikes a person or building, the molecular movement on the surface increases, causing a sensation of warmth. If energy moves away from the body by evaporation or cold air, for

THE ELEMENTS THAT MAKE UP
YOUR MICROCLIMATE

Temperature	winter and summer duration of hot and cold weather
Sun	direction in winter and summer height in summer and winter angle of sunset and sunrise in winter and summer
Wind	direction of prevailing wind in winter and summer direction of frequent storm winds direction of hurricane winds
Frequency of *Storms*	what kinds, winter and summer
Rainfall	how much in winter and summer direction of water runoff location of wet and dry spots
Snowfall	how much in winter direction of snow drifts
Humidity	winter and summer
Radiation of Heat *from Ground to Sky*	at night from buildings, water and land
Absorption of Heat *from Sky to Ground*	during day by buildings, water, and land
Topographical Features	mountains, lakes, valleys, plains, woods
Site	rolling, sloping, level, dry, wet
Ground Surfaces	concrete, blacktop, grass, other
Building Surfaces	stone, brick, concrete, wood, aluminum, other
Roof	color, slope

example, there is a decrease of molecular movement and a sensation of cold is noticed. Human comfort is not determined solely by air temperature. Humidity, evaporation, and wind chill are also involved in the sensation of a pleasant climate. This is called the *human comfort zone.*

The variables that affect the human comfort zone are temperature, humidity, air movement, and radiation. They may be adjusted independently or simultaneously, to provide the most pleasant atmosphere.

RELATIVE HUMIDITY

Relative humidity at a specific temperature is the ratio of the actual amount of moisture in the air compared to the amount it potentially could hold. The relationship, expressed as a percentage, is crucial to the sensation of comfort. Evaporation from the skin makes us feel cooler. At low temperatures, relative humidity is less important than the actual thermometer reading. When a relative humidity of 60 percent or more coincides with a temperature above 65 degrees F. it feels uncomfortable, muggy, and humid. In a dry climate, the same temperature would not be uncomfortable.

Under humid conditions, breezes evaporate moisture from the skin, removing heat from the body. In hot-humid climates, air flow indoors and outdoors is as important to human comfort as is the temperature. Breezes are measured by recording wind velocity and direction. Summer winds, properly directed by site topography or vegetation or both, can reduce the need for air conditioning.

Controlling the variables to produce conditions closer to the human comfort zone is what this book is about. By modifying the vegetation, terraces, walks, walls, fences, and land forms, you can decrease temperature fluctuations indoors. Less fossil fuel is needed. Dollars can be saved on heating and cooling.

MECHANISMS OF HEAT LOSS AND GAIN

In order to use plant material and land forms effectively for energy savings, you must first understand how heat energy is transferred and how the transfer affects us. Each mode of energy exchange responds to specific techniques. For instance, it is useless to spray water into the prevailing wind to cool a house, if the hose nozzle is downwind from the building. It would just increase your water bill.

Heat loss and gain follow four main routes in buildings: 1) conduction, 2) convection, 3) radiation, and 4) evaporation.

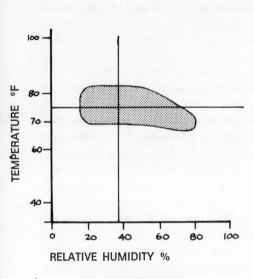

▲ **A STANDARD COMFORT ZONE**

IN ORDER TO FEEL COMFORTABLE ▶

1 A PERSON SITTING IN THE SHADE
   NEEDS AIR IN THE "STANDARD"
   COMFORT ZONE
2 A PERSON RUNNING IN THE SUN
   NEEDS COOLER, DRIER AIR
3 A PERSON SITTING IN THE SUN
   NEEDS COOLER AIR
4 A PERSON SITTING IN THE SHADE
   IN A COOL BREEZE NEEDS WARMER
   AIR

Human Comfort Zone

Conduction loss is through walls, floors, foundations, ceilings, from the surfaces themselves, directly.

Convection heat loss is through leaks where air can escape, such as loose doors and windows. The stronger the wind blows, the more heat is lost by convection. (Proper windbreaks can reduce the wind by up to 85 percent.)

Radiation heat exchange takes place through glass. During the day, sun warms the inside of the house. Black night skies draw heat from interiors to the outside.

Evaporation of water vapor uses energy to produce its cooling effect. Evaporation heat exchange is why trees and plants have so much cooling effect.

BUILDING MATERIALS

Heat is absorbed differently by different building materials, and by plants. Terraces, walls, driveways and pools are all made of building materials but are part of the landscaping. Also, the material of which the house is made has considerable effect on the heat absorption and radiation patterns of the yard.

Because heat is absorbed differently by the different substances, small pockets with widely different temperatures are created in the yard. These microclimates often vary from one side of the building to another.

Some materials, generally those with light-colored surfaces, reflect light and heat. Some materials (such as a white wall on a house) reflect and send the heat back into the air, while keeping the space behind them cool. But in the South, white walls and terraces may reflect enough sunlight onto outdoor living areas to make them too bright and too hot. Shade is needed during the heat of the day.

Some materials absorb energy from the sunlight and remain cool. A tree is a good example. Leaves absorb energy in the blue and red spectrum of light. They do not use green light as much, but they reflect this part of the spectrum and so appear green. There is practically always a pleasant breeze under trees as their leaves evaporate water. As leaves evaporate water vapor, air currents are produced, creating a wind chill factor, which makes the air feel even cooler.

Some materials absorb energy and get hot. A blacktop driveway becomes hot in the sun. It absorbs a great deal of the sun's

light but doesn't use any of this energy for evaporation or meta-
bolic processes. Blacktop is preferred in areas that have snow
because snow melts and evaporates faster on blacktop than on
concrete.

NIGHT TEMPERATURES—RADIATIONAL COOLING

At night, heat energy that has been absorbed during the day
by the ground, by masonry, and by buildings is radiated up into
the black sky. Its direction is exactly opposite of the sunlight energy
that radiates down during the day. In dry areas that have cloudless
skies, there can be enormous radiational cooling at night. It is
difficult to comprehend the magnitude of nighttime radiational loss
when skies are clear. Though an area may have an air temperature
of 95 degrees F. at noon, the temperature by sunset is likely to be
about 75 degrees F. and by 5 a.m. may fall as low as 28 degrees F.

Buildings and masonry that absorb heat from sunlight will
cool slowly at night, keeping the area warmer. In desert areas,
with chill nights, it is useful to have masonry, rocks, and concrete
near the house. In cities, however, the low overhead smog prevents nighttime radiational cooling. The heat just hangs there.
Cities, in both winter and summer, are warmer than their green
suburbs. The city buildings, sidewalks, and streets absorb massive

Temperatures in the Yard

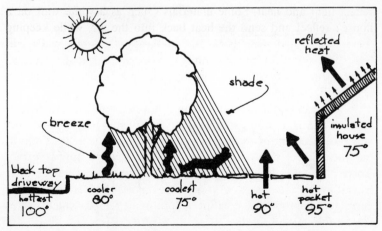

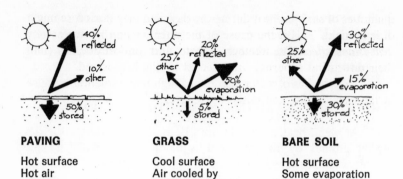

PAVING

Hot surface
Hot air

GRASS

Cool surface
Air cooled by
high evaporation

BARE SOIL

Hot surface
Some evaporation

Different Absorption of Heat by Different Surface Materials

Radiational Cooling

Moisture lowers the effective night heat loss. Dry, clear air increases it.

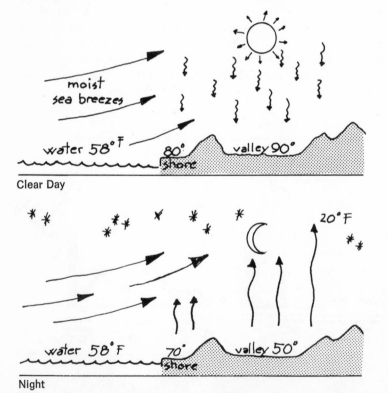

Clear Day

Night

quantities of sunlight-heat during the day, and they don't lose much of it at night. This is the cause of the phenomenon known as city *heat-island effect*. The weather, climate, and comfort of cities (and their downwind suburbs) are affected by the heat-island.

Large bodies of water also retard nighttime radiation because of the frequent fog and mists they cause.

2

THE SUN

The sun is the source of all energy. Obviously then, the more sunlight hitting and entering a building in summer, the higher the cost of air conditioning. The opposite is true in winter with heating costs.

A simple way to block summer sun and admit winter sun is to plant a carefully placed deciduous tree, one that loses its leaves in autumn. It will provide shade in summer, and yet in winter the warming sun will pass through its leafless branches.

But proper placement is not so simple. The relation of earth and sun changes with the seasons. The earth rotates once a day on its own axis. It also rotates around the sun once each year. As it does, first the northern, then the southern portion of the earth gets the direct rays of the sun. In summer, the northern hemisphere is toward the sun, so days are longer. The sun is higher in the sky. In winter, the converse is true.

Because of this seasonal tilt, the angle of the sun on any given day is different at each latitude and during each season. Although in the northern hemisphere the sun is always to the south at noon, it may be high in the sky (summer) or low on the horizon (winter).

THE SEASONS

Ancient civilizations were fascinated with astronomy. High priests did secret calculations to predict where the sun would rise and how high it would be in the sky. They fashioned religions based on sun worship. Abu-Simbel, the great temple on the Nile, is oriented to the sun in an extraordinarily sophisticated fashion. On one day of the year, the rising sun shines exactly through the small door, lighting the whole inside. The shaft of light precisely illuminates the statue of the sun god, Amun-Re, at the very back wall.

In England, there is Stonehenge. It stands as a silent memorial to a simple people who immortalized the spring equinox in granite monoliths. When their sun rose between a narrow slit in the sacred circle of stones, it was time to plant the crops—the eternal, vernal equinox. Stonehenge has other liths. They plot other sunrises, even moonrises, catching forever their variations during the changing seasons.

Today we have a calendar that tells the day, the month, and when to plant the tomatoes. It's very worthwhile for the cost-conscious homeowner to figure the different angles of the sun for efficient energy savings. Planting by gosh and by golly will help some. But why waste good plant material by using it ineffectively?

Sun and Shade

summer sun

winter sun

A stategically placed deciduous tree keeps out summer sun, lets in winter sun.

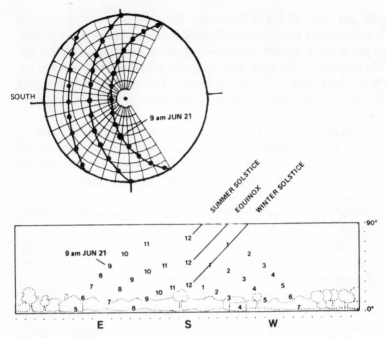

Sun Path Diagram

A Sun-path diagram, latitude 40 North, is a circular graphic "map" of the elevation of the sun at all hours of the day for each day of the year. Note: "SPRING AND FALL" may be added after EQUINOX

A better approach is to understand the sun and shadows on your own site before planting. If you plan their location carefully, the same trees will allow both maximum winter sun and maximum summer shade.

Few houses are oriented exactly due north and south. However, if you think of your homestead as round, rather than rectangular, you will see which sides benefit or suffer from sun. Then just apply the same principles to those exposures.

DIRECTION AND ANGLE OF THE SUN

A breakdown of the changes in direction and angles of the sun during the year in your latitude is available (with difficulty) from your weather bureau. Or you can easily plot them yourself.

Place a six-foot stick in the center of an open area. Record the length and direction of the shadows during one full day in

July and one full day in December. Measure at 9 a.m., noon, and 3 p.m., also at 6 p.m. during July. Record the shadows on a large paper collar that's slit to fit around the stick. The marked collar will help you to situate future trees and will be a permanent record. (It can also serve as a sundial clock in a pinch.) The direction of the shortest shadow is a true North-South axis, daylight-savings time notwithstanding.

Since six feet is generally the height of a sliding glass door, the length of the shadow will tell how far the sun will reach inside the house through the glass. It will also enable you to establish the dimension of a trellis or overhang to keep the sun out in summer.

To plan for the most efficient use of sunlight and warmth, you must first know the direction and low angles of the winter sun. Heat from sunlight is effective only between 9 a.m. and 3 p.m. So while the sunrise and sunset are interesting and beautiful, the important calculations concern only midday.

But when you make summer calculations you must make an exception for the late, low-angled, western sun during hot seasons. Buildings are at their hottest by then, and *any* additional heat is unwanted.

It is easy to calculate the angle of the sun from the length of the shadow and the height of the stick. Make a triangle on paper.

Controlling the Sun For Heating and Cooling

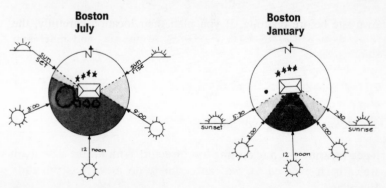

HOT SUN   Should be shaded in summer, used to warm in winter
INEFFECTUAL SUN
DECIDUOUS TREES   for shade
EVERGREEN TREES   for windbreaks; no sun ever comes from the north

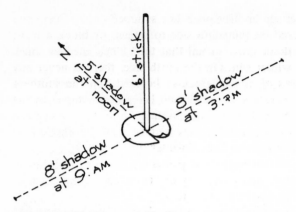

Measuring the Sun and Shadows

Put a small paper collar around the 6-foot
stick. On it, record the direction and length
of the shadows at different times of day. Use
a separate collar for each season. Be sure
collar is always correctly oriented to points
of compass.

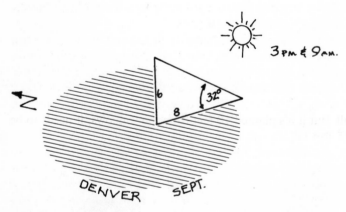

To Measure the Angle of the Sun

Then measure the angle using a protractor. With all the new math
we've been exposed to, we can certainly do as well as the early
Egyptians.

PLANTS FOR SUN CONTROL

Using these calculations, you can choose optional planting
sites and varieties. Deciduous trees are useful both for admitting

rays of the winter sun and for providing summer shade. Evergreen plants may be used on the south side to screen, or block a view, as long as they don't grow so tall that they block the low angle of the desirable winter sun. On the north side, there is never any sun, so evergreens of any height may be used. On the southern exposure, fences may also be used, their heights determined by the distance from the building. For instance, a 6 foot evergreen rhododendron or a 5 foot fence may be placed 20 feet in front of a sliding glass door with no loss of winter sun.

Obviously, the mature size of plants is a major consideration. Choosing the proper genetic variety or "clone" is as important as the calculations on where to place it.

The more carefully you plan the planting, the better it will function. In summer you'll want protection on the Western exposure from the hot afternoon sun. In winter, no effective sun comes from that quarter. The tree can be evergreen or deciduous.

The taller the trees the better. They will shade not only the windows but also the roof. The majestic trees we normally think of as "shade trees" are fine, but not too near the foundation, please. These giants would soon interfere with water pipes, foundations, landscape plantings, and gutters.

Trees on the southern exposure have to shade only a small angle of high summer sun. For that reason, fast-growing or columnar trees may be used. It is interesting to note that a tree at 25 feet from a building must be over 50 feet tall to provide shade on the south side in summer. It takes a long time to grow a tree that tall. But if it's planted 10 feet from the windows, it needs to be only 25 feet tall.

Many acceptable trees remain a proper size and are attractive for planting near buildings. They will provide shade for south-facing windows or walls (see List of Small and Medium Trees, Chapter 15). Planting trees with invasive roots too near the house is asking for trouble (see List of Fast-growing Trees, Chapter 15).

On the southern exposure, lower branches are not necessary for shade. Trees can be trained to grow tall, with high space under them. This treatment gives a feeling of spaciousness and opens a view. It takes several years to develop a high canopy of leaves, but in the end, it is worth the effort. Columnar, upright trees function well because they naturally grow tall and not too wide, without special pruning. A clump or row of them (especially flowering crabapples or cherries) is highly attractive (see List of Columnar Trees, Chapter 15). Narrow, upright trees are also useful in places

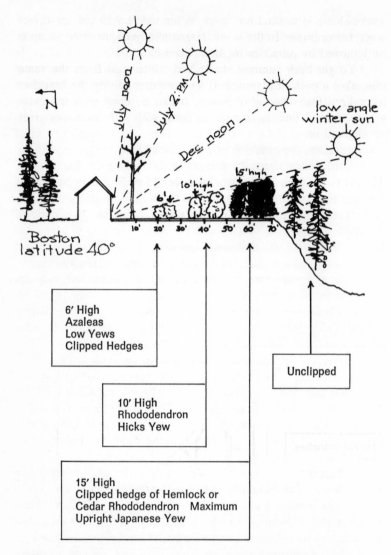

Heights of Trees and Evergreens for the Southern Exposure

EVERGREENS: Maximum mature height is determined by the low angle of the winter sun, on the south side. (Since there is no sun from the north, any height is acceptable on that side.)

DECIDUOUS: Height determined by high summer sun. Lowest branches determined by low winter sun, for maximum efficiency, although sun will go through bare branches with only a 25 percent loss of energy.

where shade is needed but space is limited: courtyards or drive-ways, for example. In the South, large palm trees are often success-fully moved by nurseries for this purpose.

To get both summer shade and winter sun from the same tree takes a peck of planning. It also requires raising the branches to make a high canopy of leaves. It can be done with tall ever-greens in hot climates. It can be done with tall deciduous trees in northern areas.

Actually, the branches of a deciduous tree, though leafless in winter, still block about 25 percent of the sun's heat. Ideally, the thickest part of the branch structure should be in the top, where it will not block sunlight to windows. Of course, it will still block some warming sun from the roof in winter. Most energy-conscious

Size of Trees to Shade Western Exposure

Object: Keep out hot, low-angled summer sun. Trees may be decid-uous or evergreen, because effective warm winter sun never gets this far west.

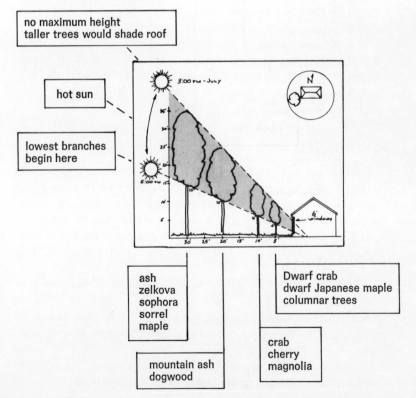

no maximum height
taller trees would shade roof

hot sun

lowest branches
begin here

ash
zelkova
sophora
sorrel
maple

mountain ash
dogwood

Dwarf crab
dwarf Japanese maple
columnar trees

crab
cherry
magnolia

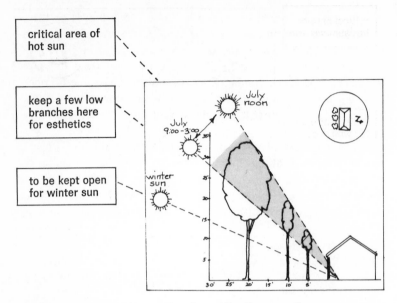

Height of Trees For Protection from Hot Summer Sun
Object: Let in winter sun. Keep out summer sun.

homeowners have heavy insulation under the roof, so it is less warmed by the winter sun than are windows. Snow on the roof is an excellent natural insulator. The longer it remains before it melts, the more useful it is.

OVERHANGS

Trellises and overhangs may be used for blocking sunlight in summer. Although trees cool an area by methods more complex than simple shading, sometimes there just is no place for a tree. A short overhang or awning will allow winter sun to enter but will keep out summer sun. A trellis with vines will do the same thing. Vines grow fast and provide cover the first year (see List of Vines, Chapter 15.)

One big advantage of overhangs or trellises is that they provide welcome shade fast while you wait for trees to grow. A combination of solid overhang and a trellis is often used. In southern climates, a deep overhang allows the windows to be kept open during rainstorms, thereby cooling the interior. The usual overhang for simple summer sun control is about 3 feet deep. In very northern climates, it may need to be a little deeper.

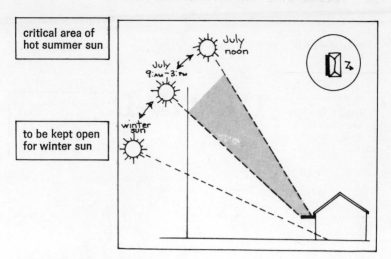

Overhangs and Trellises

Object: Let in winter sun. Keep out summer sun. In south, sun is higher so trellis may be less deep from house to outer edge.

CHAPTER

3

THE WIND

The most overlooked aspect of energy saving is control of the wind. Yet wind is the easiest factor to manage with landscape techniques. You control it by using trees, shrubs, and hedges. Equally effective are earth forms such as hills, berms, and canyons, which form baffles or channels as the need may be.

WIND FUNNELS

A funnel of tall hedges that channel the prevailing wind can provide constant, natural "air conditioning." As the funnel narrows, wind velocity increases, making the arrangement more effective. A large scoop that narrows considerably can increase prevailing winds that are light, but steady and would otherwise be ineffectual. If the narrowest end of the funnel is covered by a breezeway or a high-canopied tree, the effect improves.

Wind funnels are complicated to design. Universities test designs by using expensive wind chambers, with tiny buildings carefully built to scale. For home analysis, a smoky fire in a garbage can is cheaper though it may not endear you to the fire chief.

Wind patterns around a building can be traced in northern areas by watching the way snow blows. Make your first observation after a fresh snow, when all is white and serene. Wait a few days and see where the wind has blown channels and paths. Where is the ground blown bare? Where has the snow piled in drifts?

WIND CHILL FACTOR

Wind contributes to the comfort "temperature" as much as any other factor. In hot climates, wind cools the skin through body evaporation and by carrying heat directly away from the body. In cold weather, the dangerous "wind-chill factor" is well documented. At 20 degrees F. a hiker can develop a frostbitten nose if the wind speed is 40 miles per hour. But even at a chilly 10 degrees F. his nose will be safe when the air is still.

At 70 degrees, an 18-mile-per-hour wind can make the air temperature feel like 58 degrees. Just walking creates a wind flow equal to 4 miles per hour. Buildings suffer from wind chill too. As cold air swirls around them, the furnace must produce more heat to compensate. Winter windbreaks can reduce air flow velocity by 85 percent. That adds up in fuel savings.

In hot climates, cooling wind funnels can cut air-conditioning costs. In humid climates, moving air evaporates water vapor as

Wind Chill Chart
Effective temperature that, due to the wind-chill effect, is equivalent to the actual temperature in still air.

Danger of Freezing Exposed Skin

WINDSPEED IN MPH	Actual Air Temperature Fahrenheit						
	50	40	30	20	10	0	−10
5	48	36	27	17	5	−5	−15
10	40	29	18	5	−8	−20	−30
15	35	23	10	−5	−18	−29	−42
20	32	18	4	−10	−23	−34	−50
25	30	15	−1	−15	−28	−38	−55
30	28	13	−5	−18	−33	−44	−60
35	27	11	−6	−20	−35	−48	−65
40	26	10	−7	−21	−37	−52	−68
45	25	9	−8	−22	−39	−54	−70
50	25	8	−9	−23	−40	−55	−72

well, lessening mildew and fungus problems, and the need for dehumidifiers indoors.

Wind control is divided into two parts: 1) internal air flow, and 2) exterior wind.

INTERNAL AIR FLOW

Control of internal air flow is mainly an architectural consideration. It may require structural changes in a building. However, an outdoor wind funnel directed to a suitable window or door may be made with trees, shrubs, and hedges to produce a cool, drying breeze indoors. A house can be cooled off at night, often from such natural wind alone. In areas of low wind velocity, a fan or vent can be incorporated into the house's design.

EXTERIOR WIND CONTROL

Control of exterior air currents has more variables. Before you can use and control the wind, you must understand its nature. Air flows in much the same way as water. Neither takes easily to man-made detours. Air will flow over, under, around or through them. It will blow over anything not sturdily engineered.

Warm air rises. Cold air seeks the lowest spot. Cold air flows across the surface of the ground from higher to lower elevations. It settles in low spots and stays there. That is why there are mists on the gloaming and why some spots are perennial frost pockets. Farmers plant the lowland fields last. They are the coldest.

The warm air stays on top. Orchards and early crops are planted on hillsides, where the cold air quickly washes past them and settles in the valleys. The warm air remains at the higher elevations.

PREVAILING WIND

In the United States, the prevailing winds are generally from the west. But wind direction in any one spot may not be from the expected quarter. Wind is bent and bounced by buildings, trees, hills and valleys. It is affected by large bodies of water or open plains. It may sweep down into a yard as a small whirlwind, or blow right over it.

To learn the direction of prevailing winds at your house, tie strips of cloth (a trailing tab) on several sticks 5 or 6 feet tall.

Anchor them securely on the north, west, and south sides of the house. Add a stick and strips at any other place that seems windy. Keep a chart for several weeks, preferably for part of the winter and part of the summer. If spring is a windy time and also requires much heating fuel, check them too before planting wind-breaks and collecting funnels. The gales of the Ides of March can blow away dollars in fuel costs. In addition to the prevailing winds, there will be odd pockets of erratic wind in courtyards and between and around buildings. These should be plotted on your property plan.

AT THE SEASHORE

Near the coast, too much wind can be a problem. The wind can blow strongly enough to be unpleasant on all but the hottest days. In the San Francisco area, for instance, two out of every three days from May through September will have winds above 20 miles per hour. In Seattle and San Diego, every summer day will have winds above 10 miles per hour. Consider the implications of the wind-chill chart. Even comfortable days can seem chilly.

Also, prolonged buffeting from wind can be upsetting. The persistent, whistling "Mistral" wind of the Mediterranean is re-

Cold Air Flows Like Water

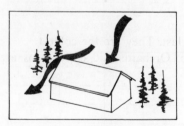

Cold Air Trapped in Patio

Cold Air Deflected by
Evergreen Trees

Corrected to Drain from Patio

Sample Wind Direction Chart

NORMAL WINDS   day   speed   weather   night   speed   weather   comments

Date 6-21	→	+	sunny	↖	+++	rain	thunder
22	→	+	sunny	↗	++	clear	
23	→	+	sunny	↘	+	cloudy	
24	↓	++	rain	↓	+	rain	
25	↖	+	cloudy	↗	++	clear	
26	→	+	sunny	↗	++	clear	
Prevailing	→	+		↗	++		

YOUR WIND DIRECTION CHART

UNUSUAL STORMS

9-23	↗	++++	rain	↗	+++	rain	hurricane

Sample location in Southeast near Gulf of Mexico, hot-humid region

KEY N ↑ → Arrows indicate the direction of the wind as related to north
+   light wind speed
++   moderate wind speed
+++   strong wind
++++   violent wind speed

ported to drive men mad. The hot, sandy "Sirocco" wind out of the Sahara has similar notoriety.

Solving the problem of too much wind is not easy. A well-anchored fence is the best solution. Eventually windbreaks of trees and shrubs can be made to grow, but they may cut off the view. Glass panels can be used to preserve a valuable vista.

FENCES

There are many kinds of fences to control the wind. But because air tends to flow like water, different fence designs affect the wind differently. Each pattern creates behind it an area of protection called a wind shadow. Surprisingly, the fence that gives the largest area of protection is a louvered one, even though the wind passes through it into the protected area.

The persistent wind of the open plains is annoying, and in winter, cold. One important use of landscaping for energy control is the creation of windbreaks to block the ever-blowing wind. In winter, the velocity of the cold air increases, unchecked by any natural impediments on the boundless space. Almost all farms

Wind Patterns Corrected for Maximum Efficiency
Winter protection screen. Summer collecting funnel. Because the exact direction of wind for each location is variable, wind screens and funnels are not oriented to points on the compass but to actual observed wind direction.

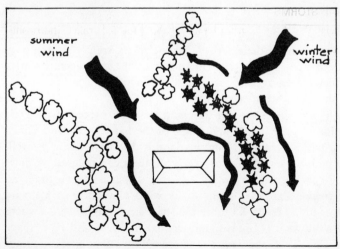

A Fence With a View
Plexiglas or glass panels provide wind protection. They may be removable for protection during storms.

and buildings on the plains have good, thick windbreaks on the north and west to, at least, create a wind shadow in which comfort is possible. Because of the persistent wind, the temperature extremes, and the alkaline soil, windbreaks on the plains have special horticultural requirements. These needs are discussed in the section on vegetation, and there are special plant lists in Chapter 15.

WIND SHADOWS

Wind can be deflected or channeled by solid objects or by clusters of trees and shrubs. On each side of any deflecting object is a quieter area known as a wind shadow. The wind is weaker there; the air is warmer.

The size and shape of the wind shadow (protected area) is determined by the height and shape of the barrier. Hillsides make the best natural barriers. Man-made hills can work about as well. Where no hill exists, walls or evergreen trees can be used. A mass of trees can decrease air velocity for a distance of five times its height to the windward (where the wind blows from). Velocity decreases for as far as 25 times the trees' height to leeward (where the wind blows to). Immediately behind the trees will be a space with still air. This quiet space is where cold-weather energy savings are highest.

DOWNDRAFTS

Downdrafts can cause unpleasant conditions in an outdoor living space. They are especially troublesome near tall buildings and are difficult to control. Ingenuity can sometimes help. The scientific way is to make a scale model and blow smoke over it with a fan (a miniature wind-tunnel effect). Then various structural modifications can be tried. It is not a job for an amateur, because the corrective structures involved are too expensive for random experimentation.

STORM WINDS

Storms produce high winds. Trees may fall onto buildings, causing considerable damage. It is best to keep all trees pruned for

Fence Designs   *Wind Shadow Protection on the Prairie*

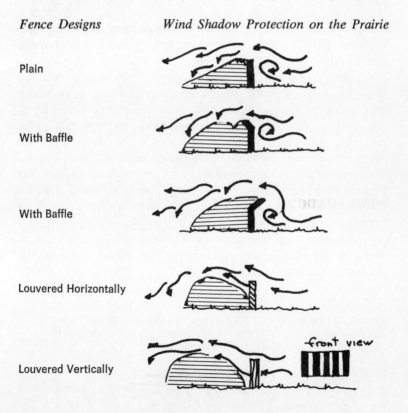

Plain

With Baffle

With Baffle

Louvered Horizontally

Louvered Vertically

front view

 Area of protected wind shadow behind fence

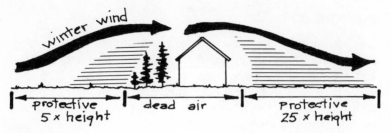

Wind Shadow
An evergreen wind screen breaks the force of the wind and produces a wind shadow both in front and behind. Dead air space protects the house.

safety to prevent storm crises. Dead wood, and weak or unbalanced branches are the culprits (see Pruning, Chapter 9). It is also prudent to plant soft-wooded trees far enough away from the house for weak branches not to fall on it. Generally, the faster a tree grows, the weaker and softer is its wood. Especially susceptible to breakage are silver maples, poplars, willows, cottonwood, siberian elms, and tulip trees. Plane trees break less often.

Most severe weather in the United States comes from the West-Southwest. Caution should be the watchword in plantings on this quarter. Of course, there are local variations that will affect the directions of storm winds. Large bodies of water modify storm direction. New England has its northeasters; the Gulf coast has hurricanes. Areas downwind from major polluting cities have a higher incidence of thunderstorms, rain, and high winds and 200 percent more hailstorms. If you live in such an area, consider planting soft-wooded trees far enough away from the house to prevent trouble.

Another protective device is to plant a smaller tree between the large tree and the house. If the big tree falls, it lands on the smaller tree before it can hit the roof.

A Downdraft
Protective evergreens and wind scoop make house and yard more comfortable on cliff in Maine. The principle of a wind scoop is the same as that of a smoke shelf in a fireplace.

CHAPTER

4

WATER

Water is the great equalizer. During summer, large bodies of water absorb and retain heat from sun and air, like giant solar storage tanks. Water cools more slowly than air. As winter approaches, it stays warmer. It slowly releases its heat and warms the surrounding land. By spring, oceans and lakes are chilled enough to provide slow cooling in summer. The seasons come and go. The cycle repeats.

The seashore in summer is cooler and more pleasant than inland areas, and shore winters are milder. The ameliorating effect of water on the climate helps give ocean and lake property its premium value. Water's absence helps explain why the midwest plains have temperature fluctuations from −40 degrees F. to over 100 degrees F. Ocean areas at the same latitude are warm or mild.

Water generates wind currents. During summer, hot inland air rises above the cooler air at the water's surface. Temperature differentials result in the familiar offshore breezes. The larger the body of water, the more effect it has on climate patterns near its shores.

However, small ponds can affect their local climates too. Very small ponds, pools, and fountains affect their immediate areas. The more total volume and evaporative surface a body of water has, the more influence on climate.

EVAPORATION

The process of evaporation requires energy or heat. It takes much more energy to evaporate water than to just heat it an equivalent amount. As evaporation takes place, energy is drawn from the surrounding air. Heat is used up and the air becomes cooler. This cooling also creates a movement of the air (convection heat exchange) perceptible as breeze or wind. At ocean or lake side, these evaporation-induced air movements augment those produced by the simple thermal differentials of the air and water.

Homeowners can use these energy-exchange phenomena to their maximum advantage by incorporating both plants and water into their garden designs.

No great classic garden or outstanding retreat is without some water. The tranquil surface of ever-changing light, as well as the sound of running, gurgling water, have universal esthetic appeal.

PLANT MATERIAL

All plants, especially trees, are good for harnessing the water-evaporation energy-exchange cycle. In addition to cooling by shade, trees also cool by evaporation of water from their leaves. The energy required for this evaporative process is taken out of the air as heat. As air temperature differentials develop, convection currents are set up. These draw air through the leaves and create the breeze that is nearly always under large trees.

THE TREE FACTORY

In fact, the combination of shade, evaporation, and convection air currents can lower the temperature beneath big trees by 25 degrees. One mature tree produces as much cooling as five 10,000 BTU air conditioners. Trees also collect pollutants and particulate ash from the air. While trees metabolize, they remove carbon dioxide from the air and manufacture oxygen, especially needed in urban areas with poor air quality. Trees give a great deal in exchange for just dirt and water.

For the homeowner in a sultry climate, large trees are worth their weight in electric bills. A grove of trees will always provide a cooler spot. The higher the temperature, the more leaf surface is needed to produce enough cooling. Also the higher the leaf canopy needs to be to provide maximum air movement.

If a tree is expected to cool the climate, it must have adequate water at all times, and lots of leaves. If the ground dries, trees don't have as much water in their leaves to give off, nor ground water in their roots to replace what they lose.

Unfortunately, desert plants expose a minimum of leaf surface to protect themselves from drought and prevent evaporation and water loss. Where adequate irrigation isn't possible because of water restrictions, drought-resistant trees must be used. They will still provide shade, but much less evaporation of water will take place from their leaves.

As evaporation takes place, the resulting energy (heat) loss makes a person, a building, or any object feel cooler. It explains the old desert trick that keeps water cool. Water is stored in a canvas bag or porous clay jug. In both instances, the outside surface stays wet. Water evaporates from the surface and in the process draws heat from the water inside. The drinking water stays cool. There are no refrigerators on camels or in Bedouin back yards.

Traditionally, hot courtyards always had fountains. In dry climates, an increase of humidity is especially welcome to people, plants, and good furniture. Man-made lakes, pools, and fountains can be used to advantage where no ocean or lake exists naturally. For maximum effects, they should be placed upwind to both cool and humidify the largest area.

The amount of evaporation is directly related to the amount of surface area. A spray or fountain exposes more surface than still water. A similar cooling effect can be created by wetting or hosing down a patio, driveway, or roof. Roofs can have sprays or just running water over them, for evaporative cooling. In very hot climates, a shallow water pool on the roof provides considerable energy saving. As the water cools at night, it becomes a cool blanket ready when the next day heats up again. It evaporates during the day, drawing heat energy from the building.

In climates with hot sun but chilly nights, water roofs are warm and insulative. So is sod on the roof. Thatch provides insulation too, but it does not provide evaporative cooling during day.

Irrigating with Rainwater

1. Roof runoff water
2. Drain pipes
3. Hot paved area cooled with surface runoff
4. Trees and grass irrigated with surface runoff
5. Shrubs irrigated with surface runoff
6. Irrigation under overhang; perforated pipe on crushed stone
7. Perforated pipe under tree roots
8. Irrigating vegetable garden from end of pipe

CONSERVING WATER

Too often roof rainwater runoff is channeled into the ground via sewer or dry well. The old rainbarrel was no joke, just common-sense conservation. Roof water can be used. It can go from the drainpipe through a small pool or fountain, or over paved areas in hot, frost-free climates. It can be used first for these cooling purposes, and then used again for irrigation. Perforated underground "Bemco" pipes can distribute it under tree roots and shrubbery beds. Finally the water can be directed to the vegetable garden. Clean waste water from sinks and bathtubs can be used similarly for underground irrigation. (Using water heavily contaminated with detergents should be avoided until more is known about salt and mineral buildup.)

In Shalimar, the unbelievably beautiful Persian Garden of Love, water from the Himalaya mountains runs down a series of terraces. At each level, it irrigates the flower beds, charges the fountains, and fills the wading pools. Then it falls a few feet to the next terrace to work again.

Uncomplicated irrigation systems, such as this, using either pipes, crushed stone, or directed surface runoff, can save water bills, produce better trees and shrubs, and occasionally help with evaporative cooling. Under roof overhangs, this kind of irrigation can help you avoid sickly shrubs and high water bills.

A word of caution: if you plan to build a small ornamental pool or fountain, don't use ground runoff water. It usually has silt and debris in it. However, roof water is clean and usable after it's run through a screen. Goldfish or a thin coat of cooking oil will control mosquito larvae.

SNOW

Snowfall patterns can be useful for saving energy too. Snow is an insulating material in cold climates. When it stays on the roof, heating costs are lower. Similarly, when it piles against a north or windy wall, particularly when held by shrubbery, it protects that wall from wind chill and low temperatures.

Snow blowers can be directed to blow on exposed walls, or to create large mounds that serve as temporary windbreaks. In open areas, like in the prairie states, the use of carefully placed shrubs or snow fencing can catch and hold snow blown by winter winds. It may require a season of watching the wind, and some trial and error, before you find the best locations.

5

LAND FORMS– NATURAL AND MAN-MADE

NATURAL LAND FORMS

The surface of the earth is wrinkled by shapes that we call hills, valleys, canyons, and ridges. These land forms affect our climate. They modify the wind and sun-light, form cold and hot spots, and determine which trees and shrubs will grow. By so doing, they influence how much it costs us to make the microclimate of our own backyard comfortable.

Mountains, for instance, force the wind around or over them, into erratic gusts and swirls. Rainfall is affected. Hills do the same to a lesser degree. Canyons and narrow passes constrict the wind, increasing its velocity or "wind speed." The faster it blows, the cooler it feels. Sometimes it blows too hard.

HILLSIDES AND VALLEYS

Because cold air flows much like water from higher to lower elevations, hillsides have special climates. Cold air tends to flow down their sides into the valleys. The middle elevations of hills and mountains are more comfortable and most energy-conservative. Cold air flows right through middle elevations. The night air is often warmer than the air in the valley. Because there usually is some breeze on hillsides, hot days are cooler. The top and side of a hill or mountain facing the prevailing winds, are always colder. Orchards prefer the middle elevations, where extremes of temperature are less likely.

Valleys may be hot if their sheltering hills are broadside to the prevailing winds. But if the valley parallels the existing wind, it acts like a wind tunnel and is usually cool. In the North, such a valley can be very uncomfortable during winter. It is worth considering the wrinkles in the earth's surface when buying a house lot or an existing house.

MICROCLIMATES

When air flows around hills and mountains, hot pockets and cold spots are created. They are natural microclimates. It is possible to create similar pockets on almost every existing lot by using the building, and carefully planned earth mounds, fences, trees, and shrubs. The theory is to capture or exclude air currents and sun.

In nature, these pockets determine which plant materials will grow in which spots. For instance, in nature, the north sides of mountains have a tree community that withstands wind, cooler air, and less sun (in New England, spruce and birch). Different trees will colonize the warmer south face of the same mountain (maple, beech, hemlock).

Similarly, in the home garden, different plants and trees thrive in shaded or exposed pockets. Some withstand strong winds better and are more suitable for windbreaks. Spruce and pine, for example, are more wind-resistant than hemlocks. Man-made earth forms as well, even modest hills and slopes, affect sun and shade patterns, and therefore plant growth rates.

Choosing plants best suited for each wrinkle in the earth's crust, suited to a particular combination of sun, shade, and exposure, will prove the most economical and successful approach in the long run. To ignore the limitations of your house lot is asking for trouble and added maintenance chores. You'll be wise to study the plants growing naturally on exposures similar to yours. They give clues to what will perform best for you (see plant lists, Chapter 15).

MAN-MADE LAND FORMS

Natural land forms have resulted from geologic action over centuries. However, as civilization advances, more and more land forms are man-made. Egyptian and Aztec pyramids and the irrigation systems of Babylonia are old examples. New ones are tall buildings, broad avenues, vast treeless spaces (e.g., parking lots, farms, overgrazed wastelands). These spaces create their own microclimates. More important, they create their own weather patterns, blocking or channeling winds as natural mountains and valleys do and changing patterns of solar absorption and radiation. The more men use the earth, the more we get pockets that have extreme weather fluctuations.

MAN-MADE WINDS

Tall buildings both funnel and fracture wind, creating turbulent downdrafts, swirls, and high velocities. When wind must squeeze between tall buildings, a canyon effect takes place. The wind speed increases dramatically. In some places, people have trouble walking against it.

Long, straight streets also funnel wind and increase its velocity. In hot climates, where cooling breezes are welcome, the streets should be oriented to take advantage of the prevailing winds. In colder areas, avenues are best planned opposite to the prevailing winter winds. Otherwise Main Street will be intolerable when they blow. Such winds don't help business or pleasure.

WIND DAMAGE TO PLANTS

High wind velocity is damaging to plant material. It not only shreds tender leaves but also increases evaporation of water from the leaves and twigs. Wind-stressed plants become dry and desiccated, with twig and bud dieback commonly occurring. Trees become dwarfed. Their shapes become contorted from constant wind force, and they grow away from the wind. On such trees, most healthy, green leaves grow on the protected downwind side.

Trees subject to constant blowing need more water. The higher the wind speeds, the more water they need. Without this additional moisture, plants and trees adopt a desert habit of growth. They grow slower, the trunk thickens and they have smaller leaves. They spend their limited energy producing quantities of seeds. They mature too soon and die too young. Hot sun and high temperatures compound the effect. City trees especially have this syndrome.

Some trees and plants are better adapted to resist strong

winds (see plant lists as well as lists of windbreaks and drought resistant plants, Chapter 15).

HEAT ISLANDS

Man-made objects and land forms also change the patterns of solar heat absorption and radiation. In the forest, sunlight falls on the trees. The leaves absorb and use most of it. Little light hits the cool floor beneath. Little is radiated back into the air in the form of heat. In cities, concrete and paving absorb and store (as heat) about half of the sun's energy. The rest is reflected back into the air. Everyone has experienced city streets which are miserably hot on a sunny day.

At night, concrete buildings and streets give off their stored heat. If the night air is clear, the heat radiates into the black, energy-absorbing sky. In cities, however, smoke, carbon dioxide, and other air pollutants create a dome of heat-retaining particles. Clear skies are rare. The city at night does not cool so much as surrounding areas.

So cities have temperatures different from those of their suburbs and outlying farms. Cities are hotter. A farm in southern New Jersey has the same temperature as downtown Boston, 300 miles farther north. In Lexington, 10 miles from Boston, the forsythia blooms 2 weeks later in the spring, because the air is that much colder.

This "heat-island effect" is an important component of the urban ecosystem. It affects what grows in the city. It helps determine the kind of tempestuous weather neighboring areas experience.

What does this phenomenon mean to the homeowner? It means that calculations of heat and cold energy losses must be adjusted to compensate for the climatic effect of man-made structures and the urban heat-island. The more built-up an area, the greater the effect. The more green, the less climatic influence.

STREETS

Tree-lined streets are cooler than bare blacktop. In cold climates, the trees should never be evergreen. Sun is wanted to warm the winter roadway, to melt ice and snow. Northern roads should be blacktop, not white concrete.

Southern streets should be as tree-lined as possible. Parking areas absorb and radiate enormous quantities of heat. Blacktop in the sun may reach 125 degrees or 130 degrees underfoot. The more plant material, and the more shade, the more livable the southern city will be.

COLOR

Different colors absorb and reflect differently, a variable that should be considered in landscape design. Driveways and paved areas around homes absorb heat during the day much as city streets do. In cold climates, such areas give this heat off at night, which is a plus.

In hot southern climates, however, driveways should be medium colored. Blacktop absorbs too much heat. White glares too much, reflecting sunlight into and against buildings. In southern areas, a modern blacktop driveway may look neater, but it adds to yearly air-conditioning costs.

BERMS

Man-made hills, as well as natural ones, can modify sunlight and wind. This principle gives us one of the easiest and most useful tools for influencing our microclimate. It is relatively inexpensive to create a mound of earth (technically known as a berm) to block or channel wind or sun, and much faster than waiting for trees to grow tall.

A berm that's well-designed and planted on top with trees and shrubs can become one of the important attractions of distinctive landscaping. A carefully located berm can provide privacy and noise control too, reducing noise levels by 80 percent.

Graceful berms are not used often enough. Most builders seem unaware of their existence. Berms form the basic artistry of Japanese gardens. Large, half-buried rocks and stone walls lend themselves beautifully. Fortunate are the few who can excavate for a new house or addition, and have extra earth to work with. To truly sculpture the land, it should be left with a graceful, undulating surface rather than flat and empty like an engineer's drawing board at five o'clock.

EARTH, THE ULTIMATE INSULATOR

Berms have another very important function. Because soil itself is insulative, it can be used against masonry walls as the

Berm Used as a Windbreak

cheapest insulating material. The soil layer just has to be very thick. It also must be dry since wet soil drains energy. Because water runs off the sides of berms, they are usually drier than the surrounding lower ground.

Earth banked against walls can be beautiful when planted with shrubbery and ground cover. Or earth can be held in place with retaining stone walls or railroad ties. It can be landscaped with interesting plants or used to grow vegetables and flowers. In summer, when the flowers are watered, the moist soil draws heat and produces a cooling effect. In cold weather, when no water is added, the soil will freeze and be quite dry.

Berms can be problems. If the sides are too steep, they will erode or wash away. Stone retaining walls and large rocks are useful remedies. Or use railroad ties to hold the soil. The roots of plant material hold the soil too. Rough wood chips make an excellent, inexpensive, erosion-retardant mulch. The less steep the slope, the less problem with erosion.

Soil, logs, or wood chips, should never be used within 6 inches of structural wood because of the danger of termites. The

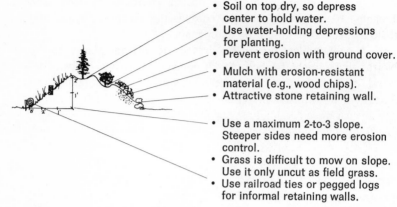

- Soil on top dry, so depress center to hold water.
- Use water-holding depressions for planting.
- Prevent erosion with ground cover.
- Mulch with erosion-resistant material (e.g., wood chips).
- Attractive stone retaining wall.
- Use a maximum 2-to-3 slope. Steeper sides need more erosion control.
- Grass is difficult to mow on slope. Use it only uncut as field grass.
- Use railroad ties or pegged logs for informal retaining walls.

Planting Problems of Berms

6-inch space should always be visible so you can check periodically for termite tunnels into the supporting beams. For new houses, concrete walls that are banked with earth are less expensive than conventional walls.

The soil on a berm tends to be very dry. Water-holding plant pockets must be fashioned when you plant. Plant material that needs relatively little water does best. It is difficult to mow grass on the sides of steep berms. Grass should be used only if it is to be kept as an uncut meadow.

MAN-MADE PLANTING POCKETS

Man-made land forms create hot pockets, cold pockets, and wind pockets, much as natural land forms do. Carefully planned, they can add to the comfortable use of outdoor living spaces, and help warm or cool a house. Created willy-nilly, they can make terraces uncomfortable and rob walls and roofs of energy.

The microclimates of these pockets require plants adapted to their particular temperatures and conditions. For instance, in a hot sunny corner, made to capture winter sun, the plants will have to tolerate winter sun-scald. They will also have to withstand summer heat and drought. For this kind of hot pocket, desert plants can be used effectively with rocks or driftwood, requiring little care in frost-free areas. Or a bed of blooming aloe, natal plum, golden rain tree, and madagascar vinca will give year-round bloom and fragrance. (Natal plum has thorns and requires pruning, but is vigorous and fragrant.)

In cold climates, a sunny pocket could be planted with Japanese black pine, potentilla, cotoneaster, creeping thyme, and daffodils. It will require little maintenance. A cool, sunless pocket requires shade-tolerant plants. In the North, these might be holly, andromeda, Baltic ivy, bulbs, dogwood, and redbud trees. Azalea kaempferi and rhododendron maximum flower best in the shade; however, all rhododendrons and azaleas need good light for proper blooming. In the deep South, a shady pocket might sport the giant climbing vine called *monstera deliciosa*, other philodendrons, creeping fig (sometimes known by its more exotic name of Zanzibar ivy), *brunsfelsia* (very heavy, sweet night odor), ginger, *agapathus*, and caladium lily.

6

CLIMATIC ZONES OF THE UNITED STATES: HOW THEY AFFECT ENERGY-SAVING TECHNIQUES

There are four main climatic zones in the United States: cool, temperate, hot-arid, and hot-humid. Each zone has different needs and therefore requires different techniques for climate amelioration.

The cool zone has very cold winters and hot summers with a wide range of temperatures (−30 degrees to over 100 degrees F.) Persistent winds usually come from the northwest and southwest. The days are short in winter with the sun very low in the sky.

The temperate zone has cool and hot seasons relatively equal in length. Temperatures are not as extreme as in cool regions. Seasonal winds blow from the northwest and south. Temperate areas have lots of rain and high humidity. The summers may be hot, heavy, and uncomfortable.

The hot-arid zone is dry, clear, and sunny. The summers are long and hot. The nights cool rapidly as heat radiates from the ground into the sky. Winds are generally along an east-west axis, with variations between day and night.

The hot-humid zone is warm and wet. Winds are variable in direction and velocity. Hurricanes are common, their winds often from the east or southwest.

By understanding the subtle differences between zones, you can use supplemental energy in the most effective way.

COOL ZONE

In cold areas, keeping warm is a task that uses more energy than summer cooling does. However, some concern should be given to relief from summer heat. Heavy insulation is mandatory. Windows on the south should let in sunlight for warmth in winter. Berms or evergreen windscreens or both on the northwest give protection from winter wind. Land forms, walls, and fences may be used to provide sun pockets and wind barriers.

Outdoor living areas are best placed on the southern exposure. Protection is necessary on the west from hot, low summer sun. Overhangs or deciduous trees on the south may be needed for some protection from the high, summer, noonday sun, except in areas with very cool summers.

The following illustration indicates use of the different techniques and their proper placement in cool regions.

TEMPERATE ZONE

It is necessary to conserve heat in winter as well as to provide cooling and occasional dehumidifying in summer.

Outdoor living areas should be on the south and southwest, protected from cold north and northwest winds. Because of the milder climate, protected outdoor areas in the temperate zone can be used for a longer season than in cold regions. Tall, deciduous

Climatic Zones

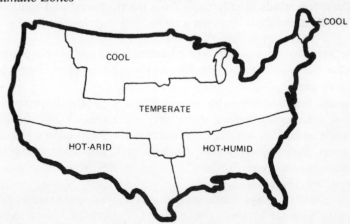

IDEAL USE OF SITE IN COOL CLIMATE

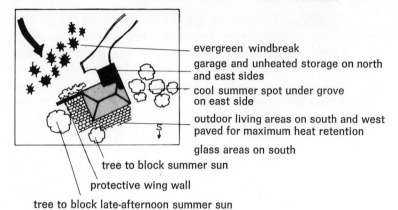

evergreen windbreak

garage and unheated storage on north and east sides

cool summer spot under grove on east side

outdoor living areas on south and west paved for maximum heat retention

glass areas on south

tree to block summer sun

protective wing wall

tree to block late-afternoon summer sun

roof overhang

earth berm with evergreen windbreak

shrubbery for extra insulation

protective wind shadow

Cool Regions

trees or overhangs should be used on the south and west exposures to provide maximum cooling, also to allow penetration of warming winter sun.

Trees, landforms, walls, and fences can provide protection from cold winter winds, where they are strong. Wind shadows should be created to protect the north side of the building and entrances from winter winds. Because wall insulation is not as common here as in Northern climates, winter wind protection is most important.

Outdoor areas should be designed to take advantage of prevailing summer breezes. These should be channeled through the house where possible.

HOT-ARID ZONE

Keeping cool during the day and warm at night are the main objectives of climate modification in hot-arid regions.

Outdoor living areas should be to the east where the building itself will provide shade during the hot afternoons.

East and west windows should be shaded. Glass walls should face north. South-facing windows need protection with a large overhang, deciduous trees, or trellises. Excessive glare from outdoor areas can be reduced by planting grass and shrubs near the building. Underplanting near the house should be thick to insulate and to hold humidity. Shade the roof and parking areas with overhanging trees.

Cooling daytime breezes should be maximized by wind funnels. In some desert areas, however, winds are unpleasantly strong, so funnels should not be considered. Instead, there should be protected areas for sitting. For houses that don't cool off fast enough at night, the north windows should be left exposed for maximum solar heat loss after dark.

Evaporation from lakes, pools, or fountains will provide further cooling and humidifying if they're upwind from the building.

Temperate Regions

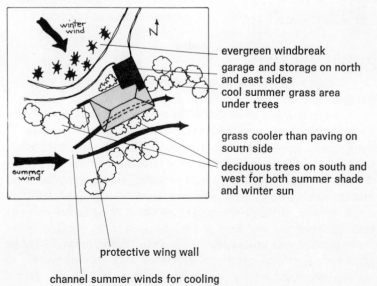

winter wind

N

summer wind

evergreen windbreak

garage and storage on north and east sides

cool summer grass area under trees

grass cooler than paving on south side

deciduous trees on south and west for both summer shade and winter sun

protective wing wall

channel summer winds for cooling

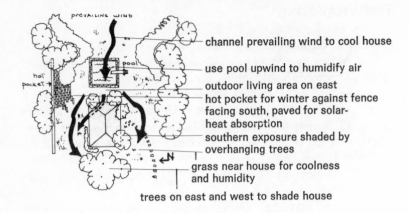

channel prevailing wind to cool house

use pool upwind to humidify air

outdoor living area on east
hot pocket for winter against fence
facing south, paved for solar-
heat absorption
southern exposure shaded by
overhanging trees

grass near house for coolness
and humidity

trees on east and west to shade house

Downwind from Lake, using evaporated moisture

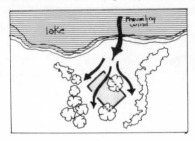

Hot-Arid Regions

HOT-HUMID ZONE

Shade and movement of air through the site are most important.

Outdoor living areas should be on the east or north sides of the building. Plantings should shade both the structure and outdoor living areas. East and west windows should be shaded. South windows should have overhangs or protection from trees.

Trees should be high-headed to allow breezes beneath. Wind funnels should be created with low trees, shrubs, and walls to direct breezes through house and outdoor living areas. Underplanting near the buildings should be kept very low for better air circulation and to minimize dank areas. Sunny areas should be grass or low, ground-cover plants. Shaded areas may be paved.

A protected winter sun pocket may be created to extend outdoor winter use.

Hot-Humid Zone

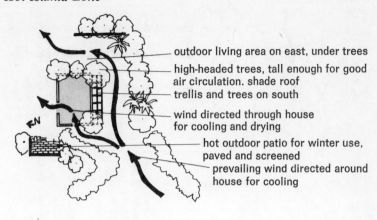

outdoor living area on east, under trees

high-headed trees, tall enough for good
air circulation. shade roof

trellis and trees on south

wind directed through house
for cooling and drying

hot outdoor patio for winter use,
paved and screened

prevailing wind directed around
house for cooling

COMPARISON OF DIFFERENT CLIMATE AREAS

	Cold	Temperate	Hot-Humid	Hot-Arid
Energy-Saving Objectives	○ Maximize heat conservation ○ Reduce winter wind ○ Avoid cold pockets ○ Maximize summer shade	○ Maximize heat conservation ○ Maximize summer shade ○ Maximize summer breezes	○ Maximize shade and wind	○ Maximize shade and wind
Trees	○ Deciduous near buildings ○ Evergreens for winter windbreaks	○ Deciduous near buildings ○ Evergreen for windbreaks ○ Either on western exposure	○ High canopy trees ○ Deciduous near buildings	○ Trees overhang roof and parking
Shrubs	○ Any kind ○ Insulating on north	○ Any kind	○ Low-growing	○ Tall and clustered
Ground Cover Paving	○ Paving near building ○ Medium to dark color ○ Blacktop for driveway	○ Grass and shrubs on south and west ○ Paving elsewhere ○ Medium color	○ Grass near building except in shade ○ Light color paving	○ Grass and shrubs near building ○ Medium color paving to avoid reflection
Outdoor Living Areas	○ South	○ South and Southeast	○ East and north	○ East
Wind Control	○ Protect from cold winter wind	○ Protect from winter wind ○ Channel summer wind	○ Maximize wind	○ Channel cooling winds ○ Block excessive winds

7

SITE ANALYSIS

Each site has its own particular characteristics, which create its individual microclimate. Making the most of the advantages of one's own microclimate conserves energy and saves money.

Carefully analyzing your house lot is essential to planning these savings. New houses, thoughtfully placed on a lot will be much more energy efficient than homes automatically oriented parallel to the street. Few older homes are oriented exactly due north and south. Existing buildings are the way they are, but nevertheless energy losses may be drastically reduced.

The important features of any lot are: the contours of the land, the surrounding area, plants, soil, wind, sun, and precipitation patterns. Before planning improvements to the site, you should understand all these factors. The following checklist will help you gather the necessary information for a site analysis (see Site Analysis Chart).

After collecting this information, prepare a rough plan of your site, showing these factors in relation to the existing building or a proposed one. As you analyze the energy plusses and liabilities of the site, think of how you can improve them by the techniques discussed in Part I. Not every example will apply to your site or your geographic area, but the basic concepts will.

The classic concerns of good landscaping design should be followed as well.

SITE ANALYSIS CHART

1. Path of daily and seasonal sun (see Chapter 2).
2. Daily and seasonal wind flow patterns (see Chapter 3—Wind chart).
3. Slope of land and earth forms which block sun or wind.
4. Low areas where cold air could settle; frost pockets.
5. Which soil is good enough to support trees and plants which areas won't (ledge, sand, concrete, etc.).
6. Size, location, and variety of existing trees and shrubs which would assist energy conservation (by blocking wind, sun, or shade).
7. Protected areas: a. at what times of day?
   b. at what seasons?
   c. protected by trees, etc.
   d. protected by land forms, etc.
8. Exposed areas: a. exposed to sun—at what seasons?
   b. exjosed to wind—at what seasons?
9. Rainfall: a. water runoff patterns;
   b. evaporation potential.
10. Snowfall and snowdrift patterns.
11. Water-flow patterns (buildings, driveways, roads, valleys, hillsides).
12. Existing impediments and channels for airflow.

THE BASIC CONCEPTS

- Allow sun to help heat in winter.
- Block sun out in hot weather.
- Block out cold winter winds.
- Channel winds for cooling.
- Use water and snow to cool or insulate.
- Use buildings and paving material for their best energy-saving potential.
- Use plant material similarly.
- Choose plants genetically adapted to perform as desired.

GOOD LANDSCAPE DESIGN

- Visual beauty to nourish the soul.
- Areas for trees, shrubs, flowers, vegetables.
- Easy, attractive access for people and vehicles.
- Outdoor living areas (porches, patios).
- Recreation areas (pools, courts).
- Convenient service areas (storage, clothesline, garbage cans, wood and mulch piles).

NEW HOUSES

Fortunate the few who are building a new house and can maximize energy efficiency. Wind channels should be carefully incorporated into the design, as well as watershed and rainfall run-off control. Simple grading and terraces can eliminate or minimize the need for supplemental irrigation of shrub borders and flower beds.

Driveways and outdoor living areas should have equally careful placement to provide the most comfortable climate and to use the materials where they will do the most good.

Building into a slope is one common, useful technique. Ideally, the side which should be protected from heat or cold is buried. The exposed side is mostly glass. *In cool climates*, the southern side should have maximum solar exposure and as much glass as possible. Build into the southern side of a slope where feasible; the buried north side of the building is then protected from winter winds.

In hot climates, where only morning sun is wanted, the east wall should have the glass, with the house built into the eastern side of the slope. In desert areas with hot days but chilly night, the morning sun would be welcome.

In hot climates where minimum solar radiation is wanted, large glass areas should be confined to the north side of the building. Windows are fine on the south, if protected by a deep overhang and from ground reflection. The east and west walls should be thick, protected, and have minimal windows and openings.

Where no slope exists, it is still possible to make use of earth berms in front of (or better still, against) the exposed masonry walls. A good depth of dry dirt against walls provides good insulation. Such "below-grade" houses have a tendency to be damp, so good cross-ventilation is important. It takes new concrete about two years to cure and dry.

Where one side of a lot has a bad view or heavy traffic, dirt berms, carefully planted, also provide privacy and noise protection (see Chapter 5, "Berms").

SOLAR BUILDINGS

Landscaping for solar buildings uses all of these same principles, except that it's complicated by the requirements of the solar collectors. Most collectors are wall or roof mounted and work most efficiently facing south. Large glass areas must be similarly placed for maximum passive solar heat.

Trees, even deciduous ones, must not shade the solar collectors. However, it is not necessary to cut down all trees. Too many architects and builders do this, incurring unnecessary re-landscaping expenses.

If the low angle of the winter sun is calculated, trees and shrubbery may be cut back (topped) instead of removed. Many trees can be lowered by half or two thirds. They then serve both as screening and to protect the soil from erosion (the most common problem on overcleared lots). Electric companies constantly cut off tops of trees under their wires. So can homeowners. When new, lower-growing trees mature, the older "cut-back" ones can be removed.

In addition, because solar houses are aligned due north and south, they are subject to extremes of microclimate. The southern side is hot and desertlike. The north face is dark and cold. Each requires plants especially suited to these conditions, and adapted to these extremes.

In addition, every possible energy-saving technique must be incorporated into site planning. The timely recovery of expensive installation costs will depend on a building that uses the least total energy. Expensive solar collectors and storage capacity are determined by total demand. Efficiency and conservation reduce the demand, which in turn, reduces the required capital investment and the length of cost-effective recovery.

IMPROVING THE SITE FOR EXISTING HOMES

Chances are that you can't move your house. You can, however, rework the land around it, as well as the trees and shrubs.

If a house needs major renovation or an addition, it's a good time to get a bulldozer and build hills and wind channels. Barring a major renovation, a load or two of loam dumped in the right place can make a good berm at small cost (see Chapter 5).

Unless you are young, strong, and accustomed to heavy labor, don't tackle earth moving with a shovel. Hire someone young, strong and accustomed to heavy labor. It will be the best money you ever spent, and may save a battered back.

Energy-saving techniques are compatible with creative landscape design. On some sites, excavating a private, sunken garden can change an ordinary plot into an exciting landscape. While not cheap, the final effect may be well worth the cost. While new trees and shrubs block the wind, the sunken garden can be a protected, esthetic bonus. The technique is particularly useful on exposed, windy sites, in urban yards, or on uninteresting land. The use of different levels can create private, protected, outdoor space.

If it's unreasonably expensive to move earth around, or to regrade your site, consider building walls or fences for climate control. Masonry walls are expensive, but they may be more esthetic and durable, so provide the best value in the end. Sturdy wood or cedar fences function as well.

The style of an existing building, its location, and the land itself determine whether masonry or other materials are most suitable. In the long run, economies taken without regard to good design are often regretted at leisure. You have to look at the fences all year, every year.

Water can be used to advantage on existing sites. Small ponds or fountains will help improve the comfort level of a site while adding appreciably to its charm. They are not hard to build. Perhaps you can do such a job yourself. The pleasurable sound of moving water is most treasured.

Swimming pools are common. If you build one on an existing lot, consider the pool's energy-saving potential as well as its recreation value. Passive solar heating or solar collectors should not be overlooked. Evaporation from a large pool can improve a dry climate or worsen a muggy one. Prevailing summer winds should be considered in relation to evaporation. They may need to be rerouted through the property. Winds also blow debris, pollen, and leaves onto the pool surface.

Ground-water runoff can be easily rechanneled to irrigate, sometimes to humidify an existing garden. (Most plants grow better in moist air.) Roof water, similarly, should not be neglected as a source of dollar savings. While building a swimming pool is beyond the ken of most homeowners, improvements to the ground-water flow are not. They require a lot of thought, a little regrading, and that strong boy with the shovel.

TO MAKE YOUR OWN PLAN

Buy some graph paper. Lay out your yard and house to scale. For a manageable scale, 1 inch should equal about 8 or 10 feet. Any complicated areas can be separate drawings, 4 or 5 feet to the inch.

Draw all the weather and energy factors (winds, sun, cold pockets, evaporation, shadows, and so on). Next draw all the landscape factors (road, good views, bad views, access, service areas, and such). Finally plot the existing trees and shrubs. Make about a dozen xerox copies of this basic plan to work on.

A Sunken Garden

Original backyard too small for outdoor living space. New sunken garden has patio and privacy. New plantings break force of wind and traffic noise. Backyard becomes usable service area.

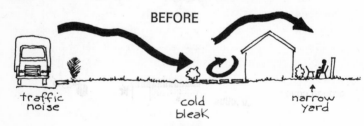

BEFORE

traffic
noise

cold
bleak

narrow
yard

AFTER

crushed stone
for drainage

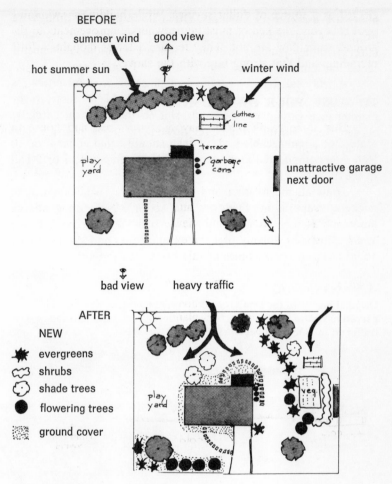

BEFORE
summer wind good view
hot summer sun winter wind
clothes line
terrace
play yard garbage cans unattractive garage next door
bad view heavy traffic

AFTER
NEW
evergreens
shrubs
shade trees
flowering trees
ground cover
play yard veg

A Sample Plan

On one, sketch in pencil what's needed. Where should there be trees, shrubs, flowers? Don't forget vegetables, fruit trees, play areas, and patios. Make several different designs, with different shapes. They don't have to follow the lot line or be square. Be sure to think of maintenance! When you have a pleasing design, begin to add the specific kinds of plants and trees to be used. Visit your local parks and arboretum to see what the mature plants look like. Garden-club house tours are helpful. Look at illustrated catalogues.

Beware of magazines. Their pictures tend to present only the very beautiful or sensational aspects of a garden. Sometimes color filters are used on the cameras. Often flowerpots are brought in just for the story. Many of the gardens are too busy with too many different things jumbled in them. Such presentations are fine for ideas, but must be adapted with caution and good taste.

A truly satisfactory garden is a pleasant peaceful retreat, a cool, green oasis in an otherwise hectic world. A fussy, high-maintenance garden will be unpleasing in the end. But carefully chosen trees, shrubs, fruits and flowers will give pleasure and soothe the soul.

PART

II

VEGETATION

8

PLANT MATERIAL–
WHAT IT DOES
AND HOW TO USE IT

Plants affect the buildings and microclimates around them in several ways. They provide shade and they channel winds. They cool by evaporation of water vapor and by actually absorbing sunlight into their leaves. The energy from the sun is used by the green chlorophyll cells to make food—the process called photosynthesis. The energy so used is removed from the air, making the air cooler.

Bare ground, with no plant material, just absorbs or radiates most of the sunlight energy it receives. It feels warmer than a lawn. It is. Where the ground is bare, temperature readings are much higher both underfoot and in the surrounding air.

The theory of using trees and shrubs for energy conservation has been described in Part I. Part II describes how to plant, what to plant, how to care for it, and how to prune to get the most out of your plant material.

The basic principles of using plants for energy savings are:

Grass cools.
Trees cool and shade.
Deciduous plants are for summer protection and winter warmth.
Evergreen plants provide year-round shade or wind protection.

Plants should provide attractive, good design with bloom and beauty at all seasons.

Plants should be adapted for their particular location (see Plants for Special Uses in Chapter 15).

Plants should be suitable for their climate zone of plant hardiness.

CLIMATE ZONE OF PLANT HARDINESS

Each plant has a certain climate zone where it will prosper. If the plant is at the extreme end of the zone, it may survive. But it won't thrive and grow to maximum size. If the plant is planted outside its zone of tolerance, it will die. Some plants die quickly, such as tropical plants in a frost. Some die slowly—they just peter out, or perhaps they lose their resistance to fungus or insect attacks.

HOW TO USE THE EXISTING VEGETATION

Every house has existing vegetation. Whether you buy or build or inherit, something is growing. It may be just weeds or a tree or two. Lucky the homeowner who finds a well-designed landscape with a sequence of blooming plants and trees that herald the seasons in an ever-changing panorama of color and interest.

You should start with the existing vegetation, whatever it is. Plants and trees in the ground have value. If you doubt it, price a large tree at a nursery. The cost is shocking. Making use of what's already there saves both the purchase price and the planting costs.

First analyze the tree cover. Are the trees useful and attractive? Next evaluate the shrubs. Are they worth saving? Finally consider the surface of the ground, whether it be weeds, grass, paving, blacktop, or ground cover.

WHAT TO SAVE AND WHAT TO MOVE

After analyzing the total landscape design and its energy-saving potential, a decision has to be made. What is serving a useful purpose? What is neither attractive nor useful? What can be salvaged in its present location? What should be moved to some other spot?

Deciduous plants are generally the easiest to move. They recover the fastest. Shrubs that have a large root system and several vigorous main stems become large plants faster. Small

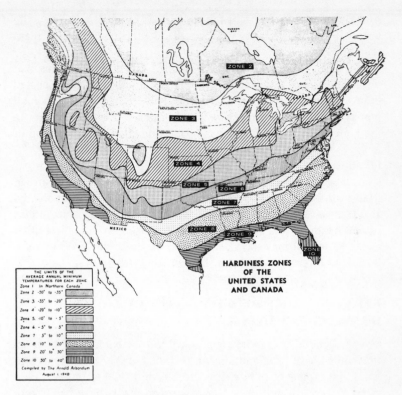

Climate Zone Chart of Plant Hardiness

trees are easier to move than large ones. Small specimens recover from transplant shock faster. They make up the size in faster growth. If an 8 foot tree and a 15 foot tree are planted side by side, in a five-year period, they will reach the same height.

It is interesting to watch an experienced nurseryman dig and replant. No quantity of written words can fully explain the nuances of how he handles plant material, or even how he uses a shovel. Observe, if you can, before plunging in.

The most critical aspects of moving plants are: 1) getting a good root system, 2) keeping the plant out of the ground the shortest possible time, 3) moving during the right season, and 4) always providing enough water.

MOVING PLANTS FROM THE WILD

If very many plants are to be moved, it is worth hiring a bulldozer or backhoe to dig holes. Then each plant, scooped up bare-rooted in a pile of soil, is just dropped in. This system is especially useful if you have access to a woodland that has unlimited plant material.

Plants in the wild often have long, diffuse root systems that transplant poorly. A greater percentage of loss is to be expected than with nursery stock. Also the growth habit of woodland material tends to be more sparse and open. After a few years in the light, however, most plants fill out. Sometimes, the shearing of new growing tips (by half) in late spring will cause the plants to fill out.

Deciduous shrubs can be cut back quite a bit in early spring. Many can be cut back to the ground, but they will recover slowly. If a plant is very overgrown, it is better to remove the oldest stems near the ground and cut the younger ones back by half. Trees that are to grow tall may have all the side branches cut back by half, but *never* the top leader stem. Expect some trees to die.

RELATIVE PRICE-BENEFIT RATIO OF MOVING OR BUYING PLANTS

In general, it is more economical to *transplant* small material that can be easily dug and moved, or valuable specimen plants that would be expensive to buy. It is more economical to *buy* medium-sized evergreens and trees. Nursery-grown plants have better root balls, transplant better, and take hold sooner. They can be easily handled and planted. Also, improved varieties, more suited to the home garden, can be chosen.

Planting labor costs about three-fourths as much as the actual price of the plants themselves. The hardest part of transplanting is digging. Most homeowners are not accustomed to digging holes and don't do it efficiently. They overdo the exercise. If money is scarce, it is worth hiring someone just to dig the holes. The mixing of peat moss with soil, and actual planting of trees and shrubs is time-consuming, but not strenuous.

Ground-cover and grass are the easiest for the homeowner to plant. However, the soil should be turned over and enriched before planting. If there are limited funds, a rototiller may be rented with or without someone to operate it. Where the pocketbook is able and the spirit weak, hire a landscape firm to do the work.

Some public-works departments make leaf mulch and give it free to citizens. It is an excellent soil conditioner and may be used in place of peat moss to mix with soil. Leaf mulch as is can be used in place of loam. Another little-used municipal resource is woodchips. These usually are free at the dump, just for the shoveling. As a surface mulch, chips improve the survival of newly planted material by keeping the ground underneath cool and moist. However, care must be taken to get water *under* the mulch during summer. Wood chips also control erosion on bare ground.

9

HOW TO USE EXISTING VEGETATION: START WITH THE TREES

Trees are the most important plants for both energy saving and design. They are expensive, and they take years to grow to maturity, when they serve us best. There is an old farmer's saying that you plant pears for your sons to harvest. Any trees that are already growing on your site are a decided plus. So start with an analysis of the trees.

EVALUATING THE EXISTING TREE CANOPY

Are they beautiful?

Do they provide esthetic values, define the lot, or screen out neighbors?

Do they shade in summer?

Do they let in winter sun?

Do they make the house damp with too much shade and too little air circulation?

Do they block the winter wind?

Do they channel air flow to cool in summer?

Are they valuable horticultural specimens?

TOO MANY TREES

Is there a problem with too many trees? It is unfortunate to remove any trees from your property, because they ameliorate climate more than any other plant material. How can you remedy the problem and still not cut them down? Corrective pruning and thinning is often the answer.

CORRECTIVE PRUNING

Trees that are too tall can have the tops cut off. Electric companies do it all the time. Technically called *topping*, this practice is also useful for trees that could be dangerous in windstorms. *Trees that are too low* can be improved by having all the lower branches removed up to the desired height, as high as 40 feet on a tall tree. *Large trees that cause too much damp shade*, especially evergreens, are a difficult problem. If you remove them, the property looks naked. The solution, short of cutting them down, is removing the lower branches. Technically known as *raising the crown*, this treatment allows the free movement of air—especially summer breezes, which prevent dampness. Also buildings can benefit from low winter sun beneath the trees on the south side.

Evergreens in the forest normally have tall, branchless trunks when they are old. There is no harm in pruning them the same way on home grounds. It retains the "pine grove" effect, but allows good air circulation beneath. Pine needles, crushed stone, or paving stones set in sand will also help an area to feel warm and dry. Grass, on the other hand, absorbs moisture and feels cool and damp underfoot. So does moss or ground cover under trees where grass will not grow.

Trees that are too dense present another kind of problem. The problem can be corrected by having many of the inside branches removed for more light and air. This technique for increasing sunlight and air circulation is known as *thinning the crown*.

Topping, Raising the Crown

Overgrown trees

Crown raised;
lower branches removed

Topped;
top branches removed;
sun reaches solar
collector

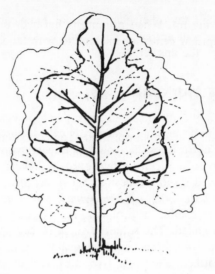

Thinning the Crown

Some of the branches in the top are carefully (hopefully artistically) removed. This process actually improves the health of many older trees. Too often people just cut down the tree, not realizing they can have both their tree and dappled sunlight, too. Branches that block winter sun from the house or patio should be removed first. Those needed for summer shade should be left untouched. The final result of proper crown thinning is an open, airy, well-balanced, safe tree. On large specimens, this is not a job for the amateur; it requires a registered arborist with proper aerial equipment.

Just because you use an expert, do not assume his esthetic judgment is better than yours. It's usually not. Don't hesitate to suggest which branches should stay or be removed. If he tells you to mind your own business, change firms. When he's finished, the tree should look attractive and natural. Too many arborists just hack away thoughtlessly.

Trees that are just poorly shaped, dangerous or have grown willy-nilly, unattended, can have corrective pruning for better shape and strength. Proper pruning improves both appearance and longevity. It should provide a strong scaffold of balanced branches. A strong scaffold means that the limbs radiate around the trunk at well-spaced intervals for strength. The branches should make open, rather than sharp angles, between themselves and the trunk. There should be no suckers or water sprouts, and only one top central leader or growing tip. When pruning is finished, the tree should have a firm, upright center of balance to withstand strong winds and ice storms.

SPECIAL PRUNING FOR PREVENTION OF STORM DAMAGE

Most high velocity storm winds come from the southwest. This is also the area where most summer shade trees are needed. Special attention is necessary for trees that might fall on the house.

As trees grow tall, they should be pruned for stability, strength, and general safety. Well-managed trees rarely fall. Usually dead or dangerous ones cause the damage. To prune trees for safety, certain danger signals are noted and corrected. First all dead or diseased wood is removed. The tree is kept with a good center of balance, with branches well-balanced all around, especially high up. Wide angle branching is encouraged. Sharp crotches have a tendency to split in storms. Split leaders are cut back to one only. Trees are lowered. All overlong branches are cut back, and all branches that hang dangerously over buildings.

Proper Pruning

Remove:

1	suckers	5	competing vertical branch
2	water shoots	6	unbalanced branch
3	excessive branches	7	weak angle, branches rubbing
4	double leader	8	scaffold branch too long

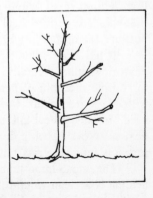

Removing Large Limbs

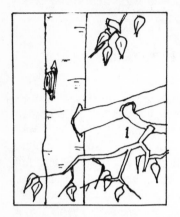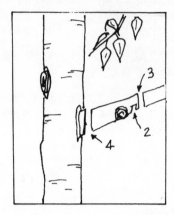

1   remove branches that might get in the way
2   undercut to prevent limb breakage
3   remove large limb
4   trim stub flush with trunk

These precautions are not necessary for all the trees on a property. They are expensive. However, they are worthwhile for certain trees close to the building that might cause problems.

Proper pruning also prevents future decay. Although tree decay progresses slowly, it eventually spreads, weakening otherwise healthy trees. Pruning cuts should be flush with the trunk, and leave no stub to harbor decay organisms. Large limbs are first cut off about a foot from the final cut. The first cut is underneath the limb to prevent tearing the bark. A second cut removes the branch. Finally the small stump is cut off neat and flush. Overlong branches are pruned back to about a half inch from a healthy, outward-facing bud, or branchlet.

It has been common practice to paint all wounds with tree paint or shellac. Actually, it does the tree no good. It only serves to console the homeowner, and cosmetically hide the raw wound with black tree paint. Creosote or house paints should never be used, because they kill the growing cells and prevent proper healing. Work is being done to develop a tree paint that actually prevents fungus decay, but it is still experimental.

The most important thing to prevent decay and promote healing is a clean wound that drains well and doesn't hold water. All torn or ripped bark should be trimmed to a neat edge with a

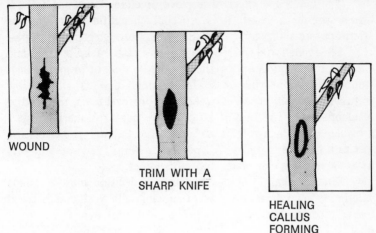

WOUND

TRIM WITH A
SHARP KNIFE

HEALING
CALLUS
FORMING

Tracing the Wound

sharp knife (called *tracing the wound*). The fastest healing cut is shaped like a football on end. A clean pruning cut does not normally require tracing. Other injuries usually do.

When trees grow very close together, their growth pattern changes. They have a tendency to grow taller and faster and to branch less. Their overhead canopy will be high, where it can catch the light. They function well as windbreaks. Rows of trees serving this purpose are commonly seen on farms.

Windbreaks on the Plains

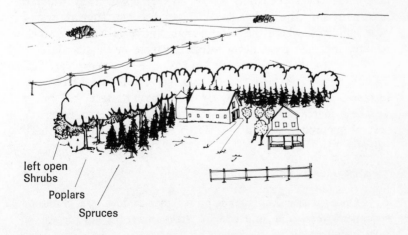

left open
Shrubs

Poplars

Spruces

The landscape effect of a grove or clump of young trees is like a woodland forest. It is especially beautiful when the late afternoon sun shines low under the leaves, through multiple trunks.

Self-seeded trees, especially maple, ash, oak, poplar, and cherry, often grow close together on the borders of property, near stone walls and in wild areas. Unfortunately poplars, which grow so fast in any soil, are weak-wooded, short-lived trees, unsuited to residential use. The beautiful Lombardy poplar is the best, fast-growing columnar tree there is. Sadly, it gets a fatal canker disease just as it reaches maturity. All poplars, willows, and some maples have roots which clog water and sewer pipes.

When a clump of trees is young, a decision must be made whether to keep them as a grove, removing only weak and diseased trees. In some places this may prove most attractive. In others, it may be best to remove all but a few, well-spaced trees.

SPACING TREES

When trees have ample room, they spread more and become the broad giants we are accustomed to seeing on rural roadsides or in parks. If only a few trees are kept, they will grow into large specimen trees. Given enough room, each kind of tree matures at a certain size and shape determined by its genetic makeup. Maples, for instance, grow to be large trees, often 100 feet tall. They should be spaced about 40 feet apart for optimal growth. Other large-growing trees like oaks, beeches, and planes need similar elbow room. Small-growing trees like dogwood, crabapple, or cherry may be spaced only 15 or 20 feet apart. They will not need more space no matter how old they become. They are useful near buildings, where their size remains in scale with the architecture, and their roots never intrude in pipes or foundations.

A word of caution: each kind of tree has many varieties. Each variety has its own genetic makeup and its own height. For instance, a sugar maple may grow to be 120 feet tall, but a Japanese maple will rarely reach above 20 feet even when it's several hundred years old (see Trees of Different Heights Chart, Chapter 15).

TRANSPLANTING

Once the decision is made on whether to develop a clump or specimen trees, the unnecessary trees may be cut down or selectively moved.

Clearing the Forest

BEFORE

defective sprouts

basal decay

improperly pruned
branches

large dead
branches

branch stub

open split

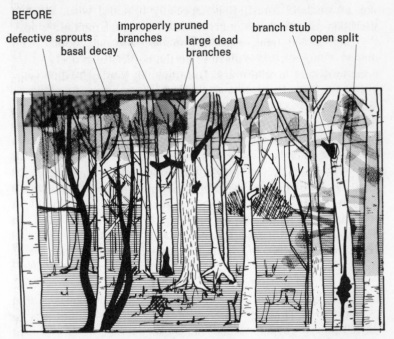

AFTER

Saplings transplant easily when dormant (before they leaf-out) in early spring, especially when about 8 feet tall. They may be moved bare-rooted to a prepared hole, carefully set at the level they grew before, and watered. They should be staked only if the area is windy, or if they have heavy tops. About one third of the top branches are removed at transplanting time. This procedure allows the roots to become established before having to support a large leaf area. It also compensates for the roots lost during digging.

On young transplanted trees with thin bark, the trunks may be burned by sun. If sunscald is a potential problem, wrap the trunk with paper or cloth. Remove it in one year.

Tap-rooted trees have long, fleshy roots, with few fibrous rootlets near the top. They are hard to move and should be transplanted only in the spring (see Trees that Are Hard To Transplant List, Chapter 15). Most oaks are tap rooted. Fibrous roots are small, feeding roots are normally near the surface in trees with good root balls. Evergreens and fibrous-rooted plants may be moved in spring or fall. A good rule of thumb is: once the buds have broken into leaf or needles, exercise great care in moving a tree. However, carefully dug, well-watered trees may be moved almost anytime, except during summer.

Newly planted trees will recover better if the soil is mixed with one-third peat moss or other organic soil lightener. A little organic fertilizer, particularly bone meal, which stimulates root growth, may be added to the soil. But newly planted trees should not be heavily fertilized until they recover from transplant shock, and start growing well on new buds. A "starter solution," which is a weak soluble fertilizer, may be used to water newly transplanted trees or be sprayed on the leaves as a foliar feeding. Strong chemical fertilizers, especially those high in nitrogen, should be withheld until the fall after planting, or early the next spring. Occasionally hormones are used to help withstand transplant shock. Almost any tree can be successfully moved if it is dug carefully, not allowed to wilt while out of the ground, planted in good soil, and watered once a week for the first year.

Caution: trees can drown and die from too much water. The roots must be able to breathe. Check the soil. If it's wet, wait to water. Newly transplanted trees use up less water than vigorously growing ones. However, a hosing of the leaves if they appear dry or wilting during hot weather is always helpful. Sometimes the few roots just can't absorb enough water to protect the leaves.

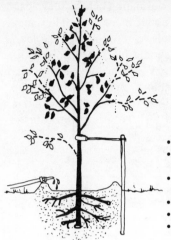

- remove all but one main leader
- cut back top growth by one third and broken or low branches
- if staking, protect trunk with wire in a piece of hose
- top mulch may be added
- flood with water to settle soil
- leave a saucer depression to hold water
- well-prepared soil with peat moss added
- roots spread out
- no big air pockets
- broken roots cut cleanly

Transplanting

The shorter the time a plant is out of the ground, the better will be your rate of transplanting success. If a plant cannot be immediately placed in a new hole, its roots should be kept moist and covered. Bare-rooted plants may be immersed in a slurry of water mixed with mud. This will protect the delicate root hairs for a few days. Balled and burlapped plants need to be watered frequently, if not daily. The tops should also be sprayed with water if they droop at all. All plants need protection from sun and wind, especially while being transported in cars or trucks.

ROOT TRENCHING

When moving larger specimens or hard-to-transplant varieties (dogwood, beech, oak and large evergreens) it is well to condition the plant. This is done by root trenching, a year ahead of actually digging it. The roots are cut all around (sometimes intermittently) leaving a root ball of appropriate size for the size of the tree. If the soil in the trench is actually removed, it may be replaced with peat moss or leaf mulch and the trenches refilled. The soil *inside* the cut is fed with a high-phosphate fertilizer or a soluble feeding solution. It must be kept moist during dry periods. Gradually the tree will develop new feeding roots inside the cut

Root Trenching

First year

New root growth inside out.
Second year

edges. The following season, when the tree is dug and moved, it will have a new fibrous root system to facilitate transplant recovery.

Larger trees usually are transported balled and burlapped. Valuable evergreen material can be moved, although it takes some skill. The larger the plant, the bigger the root ball must be. It is difficult work. Sometimes on a home property, a root ball can be dug and moved carefully on a wheelbarrow or shovel and placed directly into a prepared hole, without being tied with burlap. However burlay keeps the root ball from cracking, while it's being moved or bounced around.

ROOT BALLS

To prepare a proper root ball, dig a trench around the tree, leaving the soil around the trunk untouched. The size of the ball is determined by the diameter of the trunk.

2 inch trunk	24 inch root ball	300 pounds
3 inch trunk	32 inch root ball	750 pounds
4 inch trunk	40 inch root ball	

The depth of the ball is two-thirds its width. The aim is to get as many feeding roots intact as possible.

Make clean cuts in the soil with a sharp spade, to cut the roots cleanly. Wrap the sides of the ball with burlap and secure it with twine. (The burlap will decay in one year underground, and may be left in place.) Sometimes wire is used to hold the root ball, sometimes plastic wrapping. Neither decays and so must be removed. When the sides of the ball are secured against breaking, the bottom is carefully cut, including the tap root. (Oaks, beeches, gums, and walnuts resent this, and have to be watched and watered carefully for a year or two to recover.) The bottom of the ball is then secured with additional burlap.

Obviously, moving large specimens is not a job for the weekend gardener or the little old lady in sneakers. It requires a strong back, and someone to help. That's why using trees creatively where they already exist makes good sense. If large trees must be moved, consider hiring a good landscape firm with experienced men, cranes, and other proper equipment.

Sometimes it's just cheaper and easier to buy new trees than try to move older ones, which are not guaranteed to survive. Commercially grown trees have good root systems carefully developed by yearly root pruning, to facilitate moving. It is often hard to get enough fibrous roots dug on naturally growing trees to give them a healthy start in their new location.

Many trees that are sold balled and burlapped are actually not dug with root balls. They are dug bare-rooted, covered with soil, and wrapped. They survive perfectly well, but they should cost less than authentic balled and burlapped trees. A properly dug specimen will have a hard, firm root ball that holds its shape when kicked or replanted, even if the burlap is removed. It must be moist at all times. This proper balling and burlapping is expensive, so it's reserved for specimen trees, especially interesting evergreens and large shade or flowering trees.

HOW FAST TRANSPLANTED TREES GROW

It is a rule of thumb that the smaller the tree, the easier to transplant, and the quicker the recovery. For each inch of trunk diameter, it takes a tree about a year to recover from transplant shock and begin to put on strong growth again. A 1-inch trunk diameter tree will be growing normally the second year, but a 4-inch tree will not start to grow vigorously for about four years. In addition, root pruning (done while cutting roots during transplanting) has a dwarfing effect on plant growth and eventual size. The result is that the smaller trees will be larger than big ones in five years. For instance a 1-inch diameter maple will be taller than a 3-inch specimen at the end of that time.

Root pruning, incidentally, is how bonsai trees are kept so small.

How to Dig a Balled and Burlapped Tree

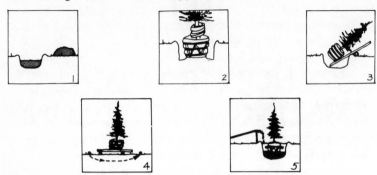

1   Prepare a new hole 8" larger in diameter than root ball. Pack bottom with improved soil (½ peat, ½ loam).

2   Dig root ball and wrap with burlap (not plastic). Wrap trunk with old blanket to protect the bark if it has to be pulled out with ropes.

3   Cut bottom of root ball. Tip tree out of hole, using plank for leverage. Small rocks may be used. This is the hardest part. Get help if you need it.

4   Roll plank on old pipes. Keep moving a pipe to the front.

5   Plant tree at original height. Remove or add additional prepared soil to get at the right depth. Burlap will disintegrate quickly in the soil. It may be left in place or rolled down and tucked in. However, plastic, burlap treated with a preservative, or metal wire should be removed as much as possible without cracking the root ball. Add prepared soil around the root ball. Puddle with water to settle soil and get rid of air pockets.
After the soil has settled, water again. Make a "saucer" to hold water. Mulch with wood chips.

AFTER CARE

6   Soak the tree once a week for the first year. Don't sprinkle lightly, or too often.

7   For the second and successive years, water during dry spells. It takes approximately one year to recover transplant shock, per inch of trunk diameter.

10

HOW TO USE EXISTING VEGETATION: CONSIDER THE SHRUBS

DECIDUOUS SHRUBS

Almost every old house has large, often ungainly deciduous shrubs left over from pre-World War II days, when they were popular. The ubiquitous lilac is almost universally present. "Lilacs last in the dooryard bloomed . . ." for Walt Whitman, in his poem, because they are unfailing, eternal plants. The early farmers didn't have much time to fool around with fussy plants, but they could count on the utterly neglected lilac blooming after the coldest winter. Usually, lilacs are improperly pruned and growing out of control.

This and other deciduous shrubs such as spirea, forsythia, and mock orange are not as spectacular specimens as are the newer azaleas and rhododendrons. But they do reappear, reliably, year after year, to give shade, greenery, and a week or two of bloom. Fortunately, they transplant easily.

They don't belong in the front landscape border. They do belong against the side and back of the house. There, especially on a western exposure, they will shade the walls from hot summer sun. In winter, the sun can warm the wall through the bare branches. Or the bushes can hold snow in their shoots, which serves as additional wall insulation. The ground and walls will be warmer under the snow's protective blanket. Heat loss from an exposed foundation can be significant in winter. In the north, snow on the roots cuts heating costs.

If fallen leaves are left under the plants in autumn, they provide more insulation under the snow. When they decay, they return nutrients to the soil. However, they have one energy drawback: they stay wet and cold late into the spring.

PRUNING

Shrubs have various natural shapes. Pruning old-fashioned deciduous shrubs is an art in itself. They should always be pruned just after flowering. Most of them set buds for the following year shortly after that. Pruning should shape the bush before bud-set. The oldest canes are removed at ground level.

When removing these ground-level shoots, you must take care if grafted shrubs, especially lilacs and roses, are cut. The new shoots from below the graft will be different from the others. These should always be removed. Care must be taken to leave a good stub of wood above the graft from which new buds can come. It should be at least 12 inches, if possible. The graft is visible as a woody knob near ground level, or just under it. The shoots from the root stock will be inferior in shape and bloom. If you fail to control them, they will eventually crowd out and kill the better grafted variety on top.

The too-common practice of cutting bushes into little balls or with flat tops is not consistent with their nature or growth patterns. Such treatment destroys their natural grace and beauty. It also makes extra work. If low-growing shrubs are wanted, low-growing varieties should be planted.

Lilacs can be trained into small trees or kept as hedges. Each year they send up new shoots from the ground. These bloom in two or three years, and will grow for many years, if lilac borer grubs do not invade the stems. The proper way to get the most mileage from lilacs is to encourage two new shoots each year, and remove the old ones as they become woody and unproductive.

Standard lilacs will grow about 20 feet tall. Trying to keep them lower by cutting them down in the fall only succeeds in cutting off the blossom buds for the following spring. French lilacs grow to about six feet, and are often grafted.

Roses, when used as shrubbery instead of in a rose bed, are pruned in early spring, instead of after flowering. They require trimming of the longest canes, and those that are too old. The new young shoots that appear in summer should not be cut off and removed. They will make the strong new branches for the next few years and will bloom the most heavily. The same principle applies as with lilacs. Encourage several new shoots a year, and train them in the direction wanted. Remove the very old, unproductive wood above the new shoots, but always above the graft. This is especially important with climbers and ramblers. Bush roses and tea roses are usually cut back hard in spring, before growth begins, to between 1 and 3 feet, depending on the kind of shape you want to produce. Unpruned roses become overgrown thorny bushes after several years, which is not necessarily bad. They always seem to have dead wood inside where its impossible to reach. Too often, they are just removed, because they are messy and no one knows how to renew them. A little pruning more often would have kept them blooming well for years. If you inherit neglected roses, the thing to do is simply cut them back hard to twelve inches in the spring, fertilize them, and be patient. A nice green mound will grow. The next year it will be covered with bloom.

Pruning Lilacs and Other Deciduous Shrubs

Lilac—before

Lilac—after

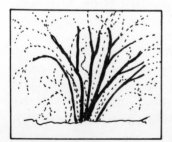

Other deciduous shrubs—
correct pruning

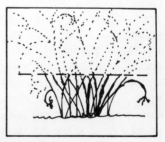

Other deciduous shrubs—
incorrect pruning

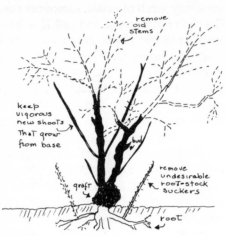

Pruning Bush Roses

HEDGE PRUNING

Hedges require a different kind of pruning, similar for both deciduous and evergreens. The hedge is kept trimmed to the desired size by shearing or clipping out individual branches. The more vigorously the hedge grows, the more often it will need trimming. It is sensible to plant material whose mature size is just a little taller than the desired height of the hedge. Planting a siberian elm, then trying to keep it six feet high, will be quite a constant struggle.

Hedges formerly were more popular than they are now. One reason for their downswing is the sad demise of the hired hand. Trimming hedges is time-consuming or costly. Some hedge material needs cutting only once a year (tamarisk, hawthorne, saltbush, saskatoon, potentilla). Some trees, when used as very tall windbreaks or for noise or privacy screening, need also be trimmed only once a year (green ash, mossycup oak, coppiced willow, beech, choke cherry). Hedges that need trimming oftener are cotoneaster, alpine currant, honeysuckle, natal plum, barberry, privet, hibiscus, and bouganvillea.

Most blooming hedges should be trimmed only once a year, just after blooming. Then they should be left to grow naturally after that, until the next year. They are forsythia, spirea, spice bush, wigelia, roses, and lilacs. They are all vigorous and will grow into nice rounded mounds, about six-to-nine feet tall.

When pruning any shrub or hedge, remember that the bottom of the bush will only remain green and full if it has light. Most people, and most gardeners prune incorrectly. Healthy hedges should be wider at the bottom than the top. They should not be round at the bottom or narrow, or the lower leaves will not receive enough light for healthy growth. Eventually the leaves fall, leaving bare, twiggy holes.

Because hedges are so necessary in wind control, understanding that you really needn't trim them at all makes planning much easier. The secret is to choose shrubs that naturally reach the desired height. Then they can be neatened up when required, but will not require constant shearing. Too many commercial gardeners from the old school recommend shrubs that make good hedges but must be constantly pruned. They are accustomed to doing it that way, and incidentally, it makes more business for them. Shrubs that withstand constant shearing, of course, must be more vigorous and often larger than is desirable on a particular lot. It becomes a vicious cycle. You're far better off to choose plants that will serve well at their natural mature size (see List of Shrubs, Chapter 15).

SIZE OF SHRUBS

The place for deciduous shrubs in the landscape is where they can grow to their full height and width. If left full and wide, spirea grows six feet tall and five feet wide. It makes an excellent barrier against cold air flowing into low spots. The charming June flowers are an added bonus. A hedge of spirea or forsythia around a low section of the property can direct the cold air around the property line, and away from the house. It can provide an effective cold-air barrier and wind screen around a vegetable garden, yet will never get tall enough to shade the crops.

Forsythia grows nine feet tall and about as wide. It can protect an exposed high foundation wall, while never blocking the windows above. It is useful on a windy, western side where evergreen rhododendrons would not thrive. Pines or sprunce would become too tall too quickly, and need constant pruning. Forsythia makes an excellent, inexpensive screen on the property border if left to grow thick and full. It likes sun, but will grow in the shade, even in city backyards, where few flowering shrubs will survive.

UNSHEARED

BAD

FAIR

GOOD

THE ART OF TOPIARY

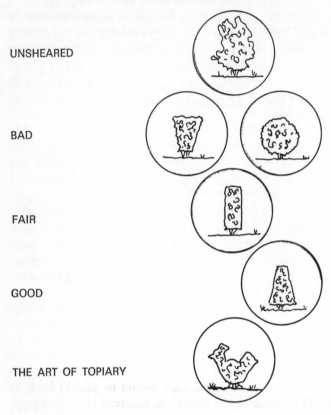

The Correct Way to Prune a Hedge

Deciduous shrubs are useful when planting double-row wind-breaks (a row of evergreens planted behind a row of shrubs). They are less expensive than pines or spruce and will outperform them for the first few years. Eventually the evergreens will grow taller, while the shrubs in front continue to provide depth and color.

Shade-tolerant shrubs are tough enough to survive as underplantings beneath tall trees, as long as they are watered and occasionally fertilized.

FERTILIZER

All deciduous shrubs are heavy feeders, although all will survive and many will even thrive without supplemental feeding.

They will use any fertilizer, inexpensive 5-10-5, or whatever else is handy. Feed at the recommended rate, either early in spring or just after blooming. After pruning hard, it is always valuable to fertilize to give a plant the food for the needed new flush of growth. Of course, don't forget to water—soak the soil well after fertilizing.

TRANSPLANTING DECIDUOUS SHRUBS

One of the most valuable traits of these bushes is that they are easy to move. Big old plants can be dug up when dormant, divided into two or three parts (each with several vigorous new shoots), and planted bare-rooted. The more fibrous root stock included with each plant, the more quickly it will grow.

Deciduous shrubs are not too hard for the average homeowner to handle, unlike big trees. First wet the soil, and let it set a day. Moist soil is much easier to handle than dry dirt. Take a spading fork or pitch axe and loosen the soil at a distance of about two feet all round the bush. Keep working it until the plant starts to loosen. Then dig it free with a spade.

You can usually tell if the root stock is big enough to divide. A two-foot root will give two good divisions or three very small ones. Cut the root cleanly with a sharp spade or saw. Cut off any dead or diseased root stock. Replant immediately before the roots dry out. Or keep the roots in a bucket of watery mud between digging and planting. The shrub tops should be pruned back by half, and old or weak shoots should be removed at ground level.

Some shrubs can be planted without big roots, given proper soil and adequate water, but it takes several years for them to become good plants. Even a bare shoot of pussy willow will root if two-year wood is planted early enough in the spring.

Plant hormones (Rootone and Transplantone) help these and all new roots get established. Best of all, the existing shrubs on your own property are free. When replanting, use the same care as with new trees (see Chapter 9). Prepare the soil with peat moss or leaf mulch, carefully spread the roots, and fill the hole with soil. Flood the soil to settle it and get rid of air pockets. Then fill to the top with more soil. Or water with a starter solution (weak soluble fertilizer) in place of plain water.

Many shrubs, especially lilacs, don't like acid soil, so if you're using peat moss, add a little lime at planting time.

Deciduous plant material sold by nurseries is often just rooted stems. It is worth paying a little more to get a good root system. Otherwise the wait for good-sized plants may be long. They are still less expensive than evergreen material.

EVERGREEN SHRUBS

Evergreen material is of two types: 1) needle (pine, spruce, hemlock, yew, cypress), and 2) broadleafed (rhododendron, holly, mahonia, camelia, pittosporum). Each requires a slightly different growing environment. Almost all are more delicate than their deciduous counterparts. Rhododendron, azalea, and holly will do well if protected from winter sun and wind. While they prefer half shade, they do need some sun to bloom well. Some of the needled evergreens, especially the pines and juniper, prefer full sun and drier locations.

Most broadleafed evergreens (rhododendron, azalea, holly, mountain laurel) and many species of pine, yew, hemlock, spruce, and fir prefer a slightly to very acid soil. In the midwestern plains and other areas of alkaline (sweet) soil, lots of peat moss is absolutely essential in the planting mix. If you're in doubt, have the soil tested for its degree of acidity or alkalinity (called PH) at your local Agricultural Extension Station or complete garden center. They will explain what is best in your area and how much is needed.

Fortunately, there is a shrub for almost every location and use. Unfortunately, near most older homes, shrubs have been used in the wrong place.

All shrubs have a mature height that is genetically determined. It affects each shrub's selling price and availability. In general, the smaller ones generally grow more slowly, and so they cost more in the nursery. The faster-growing ones (often not shrubs at all, but baby trees) are inexpensive. Many builders and unknowing homeowners planted little blue spruces and arborvitae near the house, only to discover their charming foundation planting, true to its woodland heritage, growing through windows and removing gutters.

It is sad to cut down these trees. But moving them is a hard job. After they become eight feet high, it is a job for a professional with moving machinery. Before hiring anyone, though, make sure the tree has branches all around and is worth moving. A tree that's bare on one side or at the bottom will look sparse and scrawny when moved and left to stand alone.

TRANSPLANTING EVERGREENS

Large evergreens must be moved with a good dirt ball around the roots (see Moving Trees, Chapter 9). They should be planted quickly in prepared holes. The soil should be enriched with one third peat moss or leaf mulch, and sand if it's heavy clay. Most evergreens prefer a slightly acid soil. After moving, tall evergreens should be staked for the first year or two, especially in windy spots.

It may seem a shame to buy expensive evergreens for improving windbreaks, when large ones exist on the property, but in the wrong places. It is often worth trying to move them, barerooted, which is cheaper, as long as you calculate the risks. If a bulldozer is in the neighborhood and can be hired for a few hours, the price might be right. The holes can be dug and prepared. Then the trees scooped out and replanted. However, moving large evergreens is a chancy operation, at best. A high success rate requires someone who knows how to handle plant material. The chances for success are enhanced if the root ball is big enough and unbroken, and if the plant is moved quickly. Calculate the risk versus the cost. See how the figures work out for you.

Evergreens should be moved when the soil is warm and root growth can continue uninterrupted. The best times for this are spring and early fall. Late August is the time when experienced farmers prefer to move needled evergreens. Evergreens that will be exposed to strong winter winds at their new locations should be moved only in spring. Pines should not be dug in spring after the new shoots (called candles) begin to grow.

PRUNING EVERGREENS

An alternate to moving large evergreens is to cut them back. Often they have grown so tall that they block sunlight from south-facing windows. Needled evergreens can have their tops cut right off, even by half. They will look terrible until new growth becomes full and green. But after a few years, they will be covered with new shoots which can then be kept sheared. Some people prefer to just cut down old evergreens and plant new ones if this ugly-duckling period is unacceptable.

Tall evergreens on the north or windy side of the house are another matter. They should be kept as is and tended carefully. Evergreens can be shaped or pruned to a desirable form, but kept

Before   After

Cutting Down Overgrown Evergreens

as tall and full as possible. Needled evergreens may be sheared in early summer or pruned. Shearing encourages new shoots and thicker growth. Unsheared plants are more open and informal looking.

Very tall evergreens can have the lower branches removed up to a height of eight or ten feet and they will serve as shade trees. They are pleasant, cool, and nice smelling underneath in summer.

Broadleafed evergreens are shaped by cutting off very tall and leggy branches, just above a strong bud or leaf axil. When the newly exposed leaves get enough light, they will grow, and put out new buds.

NEVER shear a broadleaf shrub like a hedge. And don't cut any evergreen below green needles, leaves, or buds. New shoots return slowly. Some plants may never sprout again from the old wood.

SMALL TREES USED AS SHRUBS AND WINDBREAKS

Small trees are the same size as many large shrubs and can be used for shrub borders or underplantings. Certain varieties of crabapple, cherry, magnolia, and dogwood will stay or can be kept below fifteen or twenty feet tall. They are inclined to have a central trunk rather than a full, bushy habit of growth. They can be trained to grow close to the ground by a technique exactly opposite the one used to prune tall shade trees. For a low profile, the highest growing tip is cut out each year. The lower branches are not removed, just headed back if they get too long. The lower limbs will absorb more food and increase in size faster. The top will have a tendency to side branching. This technique is practiced in its most sophisticated fashion in espaliered fruit trees.

Pruning Broadleafed Evergreens
(Rhododendron, Holly,
Azalea, Camellia)

11

THE EXISTING SURFACE MATERIALS AND WHAT TO DO WITH THEM

What's on the ground? It may be plant material (grass, leaf mulch, wood chips, weeds, ground cover, low shrubs.) It may not be, or even have been, alive(bare soil, concrete, paving, blacktop). What's on the ground is the easiest part of the landscaping to improve or change quickly. While the energy-saving potential is less than it is with the more obvious tree cover or shrub borders, the total effect on the appearance of the property is more dramatic.

In hot climates or during hot summers, a lawn or ground cover is the coolest surface material available. Evaporation is the reason. Cooling from any surface can be increased by hosing it down, or adding a pool and providing for more water to evaporate.

GRASS

Grass is cooling and green. It evaporates 50 percent of the heat of the sun it receives. Only 5 percent goes into the ground so the ground stays cool. Another 20 percent is reflected to heat the surrounding air. But with paving or concrete, 50 percent of the sun's heat is absorbed and heats the ground surface. Another 40 percent is reflected into the air. Bare earth absorbs 30 percent of the sun's energy, and reflects another 30 percent, heating the area. Plants alone cool it.

In the shade, grass is damp, cool, and usually not too thick. Shaded areas must be heavily fertilized and planted with shade-tolerant varieties for the grass to be lush. In the sun, grass may be brown and hard unless watered during periods of drought. In areas of heavy use (play fields, dog run, parking areas) the soil becomes packed down, the roots can't breathe, and the grass becomes sparse. Even then, grass still cools, both physically in absolute temperature and psychologically in the èffect of its green color and texture.

But grass is a high-maintenance covering. It must be mowed. It should be watered during dry periods and limed and fertilized several times a year to have a deep green color. Grass is subject to a host of chewing, crawling, gnawing, and munching animals and insects and to a larger assortment of fungus diseases.

To keep a lawn beautiful, it must have deep loam feeding, watering, spraying, seeding with improved strains, raking, and sometimes loosening the soil to let air in. When calculated in cost per square foot, a good lawn is costly indeed to maintain. And a lawn looks only as beautiful as the proportion of care it gets, which is time-consuming and expensive.

Each person has to decide how beautiful he wants the grass to be, and how much time and money he wants to invest. Everyone eventually makes his own compromise between appearance and care. A simple area of rough grass is attractive in its own way. It is just as cooling and energy-saving as a lawn of putting-green quality.

Grasses are actually among the toughest plants known. They will survive almost anywhere. It is easy and inexpensive to maintain a grass meadow with wild flowers and weeds. Such an area is not neat, just romantic. It may be moved occasionally or hayed only once a year. It is cooler than bare dirt. More pleasing, it will house birds, insects, and butterflies. An improved seed mixture for climate, exposure, soil, and appearance is the key to an easy-field of grass.

Certain grass varieties (called fescues) grow in the shade, require no fertilizer, and grow only ten to eighteen inches high. They are sparse and thin and grow in clumps. Known as old-fashioned "sheep grass," this kind of greensward can be counted on to do well with almost no care. When it gets tall, it just falls over in waves, looking as though water had flowed over it. Fescues are among the components of "Woodland and Shade Grass Mixtures." Most field grasses that prefer full sun grow two to three feet high and have coarser-textured blades. The horticulturally developed varieties for lush lawns, like Merion and Flyking grasses, need high levels of fertilizer to grow well. Investigate which native grasses are available in your area. The lawn won't be lush, like a green carpet, but it may be less trouble.

On existing lawns, a little seed can improve things. Put seed on in early spring or fall. It will thicken the grass cover. This process is technically known as "overseeding." It is worth a trip to a seed house or nursery for a proper selection of grass-seed varieties. Avoid a once-over with "Builders' Special Mix" or "Blue Grass" from the supermarket shelf.

The best time for planting grass as seed is actually very early fall. But the lazy way is to sprinkle seed at the end of winter with the last snow. The melting snow takes the seed into the soils. When it finally sprouts, the spring rains water it. At all other seasons, the soil surface must be loosened to receive the seed, and the new sprouts watered often until they are well established.

GROUND COVERS

Ground covers such as myrtle, ivy, pachysandra, mondo grass, and moss are cooling and green, too. They require less maintenance than lawns, but are more expensive to establish. They function best in the shade. In tropical areas, ground covers require occasional removal of weeds, leaves, and debris. In temperate areas, ground covers are almost self-sustaining, if good soil and adequate water are available. All ground covers, however, absolutely require a yearly weeding. Otherwise, taller trees, shrubs, and weeds will take over.

We tend to think of ground covers as low growing, but they can be any height. A good bed of thickly planted three-foot high juniper will provide more cooling in full sun than a paved area and will require almost no maintenance. Eventually it grows taller than most weeds. Its initial cost is high, but not higher than paving. For a deciduous plant that performs equally well in sun, low-growing cotoneaster can't be surpassed (see List of Ground Covers of Different Heights for Sun or Shade, Chapter 15).

Any plant material will cool the air to some degree in summer. In addition to ground covers and grass, flower borders, shrub beds, and vegetable patches are useful.

COLOR AND PAVING

The darker the color, the more heat it will absorb—and the hotter it will become. White reflects the most light and heat. It is the coolest to the touch. A blacktop driveway, on the other hand, may reach 125 degrees and be almost hot enough to fry eggs. Stone and water absorb heat slowly and stay warm in the evenings. They cool overnight and then heat up again slowly in the morning. This principle is important for dry-arid desert areas where the days are hot, but the nights chill rapidly. Warm pavements near the house mitigate the cold evenings. Then they feel cool during the hot mornings. The same principle applies to passive solar-heating systems, which use the retained heat of day.

When considering surface materials near the house, consider which is more important: 1) conservation of warmth or 2) providing a cooling effect during day.

If daytime cooling is more important, then lawns, ground covers, and the like are the choice. Sometimes where lawn maintenance is an unwanted burden, people turn to paving. Too often, they end up with a hot spot instead of the cool, easy-care area they had bargained for. A house or terrace surrounded with paving or driveways will absorb reflected heat from that paving. The paving itself will also get hot, adding to the effect. The area will be much warmer than it was before the paving.

In Southern areas, more air conditioning is required to keep a house comfortable near paving. In cold climates, the reflected heat is a plus. In the North, a blacktop driveway is preferred to white concrete. The black absorbs heat during sunny days and melts ice and snow faster.

Around solar-heated buildings, it is especially important to have the ground as warm and dry as possible. Brown wood chips are preferred to ground cover near house walls. Brown or black plastic sheeting can be useful on the ground near buildings that might otherwise be damp and cold (the plastic can be covered with wood chips for better appearance). These techniques are most useful on the southern sides of buildings where sun warming can occur in winter. A protective shield of shrubs and trees is still preferred for the north side, and any other exposure subject to heavy winter winds.

Paving can be various materials: costly, but durable bluestone and concrete, less expensive blacktop, crushed stone, and stepping stones, or inexpensive wood rounds from trees.

Durable paving materials should be set on a bed of leveled builder's sand for permanency and to prevent heaving and settling. The most satisfactory material is bluestone. Slate is good, but sometimes it splits off in layers. Pre-formed concrete paving blocks are attractive and inexpensive compared to bluestone. Color can be added to the concrete mix. Some people actually enjoy making forms and pouring their own blocks. Leaves or other objects may be pressed onto the surface of the moist concrete to make interesting designs. Brick is a pleasant texture and color, not too reflective, not too absorbent. Brick is good for temperate and tropical regions where a light surface would be too reflective and a dark one too heat-absorbing.

Wood rounds are slices (cross-sections) of big tree trunks. They make an inexpensive (though not permanent) paving. The wood has a tendency to crack and check. Preservatives such as cupernol, creosote, and waterproof varnish help. Creosote is poisonous to plants and should be used thoughtfully. The rounds, which are most attractive and interesting, may last from five to fifteen years. People who wear high heels can trip in the spaces.

Where absolute low cost is a requirement, a load of inexpensive wood chippings from a local tree-removal company will provide a pleasant surface for outdoor activities. However, economies have their drawbacks. Wood chips are not permanent. Also, there is a tendency for the chips to wash away if drainage is not correct, and they can cling to shoes. However, they do provide a rustic, adequate surface underfoot. If there are pine or fir shavings in the chips, the resins will volatize during warm days and give off an agreeable scent. Dry wood chips warm up in the sun on chilly days, but because of their porous quality never become too hot. In the shade, they stay damp and cool. They conserve ground moisture, and impart a good spongy texture to the soil beneath. Wood chips are a perfect choice under trees where sitting space is wanted, but paving would damage the tree roots.

A serious drawback is that wood rounds and chips are inflammable. Furthermore, they often provide a happy home for termites and carpenter ants, which may get into the house and cause havoc. Usually, though, there's enough to eat in the chips, without their invading your woodwork.

CHAPTER

12

BUYING NEW PLANTS AND TREES

Practically every homeowner, whether he or she enjoys the outdoors or hates it, eventually ends up buying plants. No matter how callous, thrifty, or resourceful you might be, the call of the nursery is like the call of the wild. Improving a building's energy-saving potential invariably leads there. Anyone who remodels or builds is unwittingly ensnared.

WHAT TO LOOK FOR WHEN BUYING PLANTS

The first sight of a nursery can be overwhelming. Rows and rows of plants in all sizes and shapes assault the eye. It's not easy to tell whether the plants are what you really want and need or even whether they're healthy. Will each grow to the desired size and height, in its own given spot in your practical backyard? It makes no sense to plan carefully for energy savings and then have the plant material fail you.

There are three main reasons for failure: 1) the plant is not in good condition, 2) or it is a variety that's not genetically programmed to grow to the necessary size and shape, 3) or it is not cared for adequately, at planting time or after.

HOW TO TELL WHETHER A PLANT
IS IN GOOD CONDITION

Healthy plants have good firm tissues, stiff branches, and a covering of smooth bark with no fungus discolorations, cankers, or bruises. There should be no signs of drought or "water-stress." These would show a wrinkled bark; dry, split wood; soft, empty buds; and wilted and browned leaves. Well-watered material has plump buds, wood with good "turgor" (crispness), and firm leaves without brown edges or tips. Plants may lose moisture from exposure to wind and sun, even if watered.

Check the roots for insects as well as diseases. Are things jumping or crawling on the soil? Are portions of the stem or branches wilted or black? Many a pest is imported home from the nursery on stock or soil.

At commercial nurseries, most plants are dug in spring or late fall. Therefore, buying at these seasons is more likely to give you fresh material. At the end of the summer, or at winter's beginning, outdoor plants are sold at bargain prices to move the inventory. These are good times to pick up genetically desirable stock for about half price. The plants will need loving care, but most of them will come back and thrive after an initial slow recovery and adjustment.

Sometimes you have the opportunity to choose plants in the field. This approach works best where local nurseries exist. Such places are becoming more rare. Unfortunately, most plants are grown on large commercial tree farms, and shipped for sale.

When choosing plants, look for a pleasing shape with strong stems from the base. The lower branches should have a good cover of leaves. Evergreen shrubs, particularly rhododendron and mountain laurel, tend to get "leggy" and too tall sometimes. They take time to fill out well, especially on the bottom. Some never do.

A tree or shrub should be "thrifty," which means it should look strong with good sturdy branches, not tall, weak, and spindly.

When buying shade trees, look for a single trunk, and well-balanced, evenly shaped branches. A double or V-shaped trunk is weak and likely to split in half eventually. If you must cut off too many of the branches, you'll delay the tree's growth spurt. The bare trunk should be about the height you want it. When you want a tall leafy canopy, there's no use buying a tree with branches down to the ground. Similarly, if screen planting is wanted, a six-foot trunk will be too bare.

Check the root ball. If it's soft and broken, avoid it. It should be firm and well-tied, or in a pot. Don't be afraid to ask when the material was dug and where it was grown. Will the nursery guarantee it in any way? (Most won't unless they plant it themselves.) You'll find a difference in prices. Some nurseries may be trying to unload certain overstocked items (often a good buy). But beware of unexplained bargains. In general you get what you pay for. Shopping around is sensible, so check prices and health of the plants.

USING A LANDSCAPE GARDENER

Most landscape firms get shrubs at a large discount. They sell them to you for the retail price, or what you would pay anyway at the nursery. It's hard to get a discount yourself. (If you buy more than $500 or $1000 worth though, be sure to ask for a big discount.) If you do, usually there will be absolutely no guarantee. Sometimes you can be sent inferior stock and not be able to return it.

When a landscape company offers free designing services, or other bonuses, they are usually counting on their profit from the markup on the shrubs. They make little profit on labor. The only caution in dealing with a firm that sells both plants and designs is to make sure you are not getting more plants than you need, or unnecessarily large ones. Since the markup on plants is a straight percentage, usually between 25 to 40 percent, the more you buy, the more profit they make. Some unscrupulous companies suggest more than you really need.

For this reason, a landscape designer or architect who doesn't actually contract out your work may be a very good investment. Not only will you have an impartial opinion, but the bonus of truly good professional design can't be overrated. The difference between "mundane" and "distinctive" landscaping is in the design. Both cost about the same to execute. You can usually get a simple plan for a fee of one hundred dollars to a few hundred dollars.

Landscaping is expensive. Around a substantial house, it may run as high as $10,000 to complete. A large tract may cost more to landscape. Often there is overplanting of too large specimens too close. When the plants grow, the place becomes overgrown too quickly. Annual pruning chores become a burden. Most landscape firms want their work to look good right away and to have their customers pleased, so they plant large specimens close together. Most customers do not realize that smaller ones may look a bit bare at first but would cost significantly less and would perform equally well in the long run.

WATCH THOSE PLANT VARIETIES

Better nurseries have plant material properly labelled with Latin names. On some commercially popular varieties, the label might also have a picture and growing instructions. Most labels include size and price. Rarely do they tell where the plant was grown or how large it will be at maturity.

Too often, plants are labelled inadequately or not at all. Common names, which differ from region to region, tell you nothing. Only the Latin name and "clone" (genetic strain) tell what a plant is and how it will grow. Latin names are not hard to understand. For example: a few maples:

WHAT'S IN A LATIN NAME?

Name	Genus	Variety	Clone	What It Tells You
Latin	Acer	campestre		Hardy to Zone 5–6
				25′ maximum height
Common	Maple	hedge maple		Grows from seed
				Dense; can be sheared
				Dependable; makes a good screen
				Good under electric wires
				No fall color
Latin	Acer	negundo	• variegatum	Hardy to Zone 2
				60′ maximum height
Common	Box-elder		• silver-leaf box-elder	Not a strong tree, breaks
				Drought-resistant
				Useful in Plains States
				Grows any-where

WHAT'S IN A LATIN NAME?—continued

Name	Genus	Variety	Clone	What It Tells You
				• White margins on leaves • Propagated by cuttings only to get silver leaf
Latin	Acer	saccharum		Hardy to Zone 3
				75–120′ tall
Common	Maple	sugar maple		Sap makes maple sugar
				Majestic, beautiful fall color
				Salt and drought sensitive
				Sickly in cities
				Grows from seed
Latin	Acer	saccharum	• monumentale	Hardy to Zone 3
Common	Maple	sugar maple	• upright or sentry sugar maple	• 50–75′ tall • Grow upright and narrow
				Good fall color
				• Propagated by cuttings only to get upright growth habit

Before you buy, make sure you know exactly what variety a plant is. Its performance will be determined by its genes. If they are poor, no amount of care will make it a winner. Many of the best, improved varieties are called "clones." They have to be propagated asexually to be true to form. They are reproduced by rooted cuttings or graft, never by seed. When special clones are grown from seed, they revert to earlier generations of grand-parents, which may have undesirable traits.

For instance, this has happened with the London plane tree (*platanus acerifolia*, bloodgood). The London plane is a cross between the oriental plane and the buttonwood or American plane.

Clones of Honeylocust

Each clone has its own shape and growth rate. Sunburst has golden leaves.

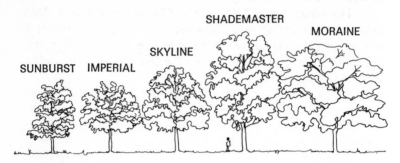

The American plane is a magnificent tree but susceptible to a fungus disease (anthracnose.) The oriental plane is immune. The original cross between them was the "bloodgood clone," and was immune. All subsequent plane trees had to be propagated by cuttings to be immune, exactly like the parent "bloodgood." However, the seeds are very easy to grow, and many nurserymen prefer the easier route. The resulting seedling trees may be like either of the parents, or any combination in between. Many are sold as London plane, but they get anthracose.

Genes are important, and reputable nurserymen know their stock. The improved varieties are more disease-resistant, flower better, grow faster, or are especially adapted to certain conditions. Fruit trees, particularly, depend on genes for taste and appearance. It is disappointing to buy a particular plant, expect it to be like an arboretum specimen, and end up with an inferior one after years of care and nurturing.

Before you buy, check the plant lists in this book, your local library, and nursery catalogues. Mature size is very important in terms of energy planning, low maintenance, and beauty. A tree that should be 25 feet tall but grows to 50 feet can block a solar collector and may need constant pruning. Where a large tree is needed, a slow-growing semi-dwarf will just never make it.

WHAT SIZE TO BUY

Small plants and trees generally transplant better, recover

from transplant shock sooner, and grow faster. But sometimes you can't wait, so you buy larger plants for more instant effect. The decision of which size to buy depends on how much patience you have, and how much money.

The adage, put a $5 tree in a $10 hole, holds true. Don't skimp on the planting medium or the size of the hole. Enrich the soil and prepare a good, soft root run for the new plant. The situation is much harder to remedy after the fact (see planting instructions in Chapter 9).

Where screening is wanted, it is wise to start with reasonable-sized plants. If a tall shade tree is needed, a fifteen-foot tree may be worth the money. The tree may cost up to $75, and you may spend almost as much again to have it planted.

Foundation plantings can cost a great deal if you want instant effect. It is the one place where a good thick ground cover like pachysandra, with smaller, less expensive rhododendrons, yews, azaleas, and hollies may be used with effect equal to a plethora of larger shrubs. Plantings of bulbs or flowers among the small bushes will create a distinctive, charming yard while you're waiting for the bushes to grow. Along the sides and back of the building, smaller shrubs can be used, also. They will not be so noticeable.

Cost of Different Sized Shrubs for Foundation Planting
(Prices will vary and can be expected to increase generally)

Rhododendron maximum (grows 20' tall)		Rhododendron PJM Hybrid (grows 6' tall)
Size 18-24" $10		$14
2½-3' 18		24
Upright Japanese Yew (grows 40' tall)		Dwarf Yew (grows 4' tall)
15-18" $ 9		$13
2-2½' 17		21
3-3½' 27		40

The judicious use of neat ground covers, edged beds of wood-chips, borders of flowers, small statues, or interesting rocks, can make an otherwise bare area look cared-for and complete. By joining all the plantings in a single bed, carefully edged, the color of the ground (plants or chips) unifies the small, widely separated bushes and shrubs. Just messy grass or bare dirt between them will emphasize an unfinished, preliminary look.

FOUNDATION PLANTING

Most people start with foundation planting. Too much money is normally spent there. It saves little energy. It is often too expensive because of the plant materials currently in vogue. Some buildings or unknowing gardeners use small, cheap bushes that will soon grow too tall. But the proper shrubs and trees that will stay in scale with the building and mature gradually, grow slowly in the nursery too. They take longer to come to marketable size, so are more expensive. In the end, they are well worth the money because they perform well. The only way to save is to buy them in smaller sizes.

One common mistake is to plant shrubs and trees too close to each other, not leaving enough room for them at mature size. Even a well-planned garden needs to be pruned back some after ten years. But pruning will become a constant chore much sooner if too many plants are put in too close.

Unfortunately, some of the most beautiful flowering trees and shrubs are too fragile to be used for climate control, except behind tough evergreens or shelter plants. However, fall color and fruit are equally distributed among hardy and delicate varieties. When planning for energy saving, beauty is still one of the requirements.

The evergreens, which are so important in the winter land-scape, are generally tough and reliable, so they can function as windbreaks and barriers. Many shrubs are also tough. Some even have attractive flowers: lilac, forsythia and mock orange; and natal plum, hibiscus, and orleander in the South. Vines are very useful for summer shade and cooling. Fortunately they're both vigorous and floriferous. Consider the blanket of bloom provided by wisteria, bougainvillea, trumpet vine, or star jasmine. The best of the shade trees (maple, oaks, locusts, gums, ashes, tulip trees, beeches, planes, and lindens) are quite tough and hardy. They peak at different dates with different colors for the fall foliage parade.

CHOOSING FOR DIFFERENT SEASONS OF BLOOM
AND COLOR—SEQUENCE OF BLOOM

In addition to mature size being genetically determined, flower, fruit, date of bloom, and its duration are also determined by genes. Beautiful landscapes have plant material of interest at all seasons in a continuous changing panorama. We tend to think just of flowers that bloom in the spring, but in fact many trees and shrubs provide color, berries, or interest all year.

For instance, the very early spring starts with pale blue jacaranda blooming in the deep South. In Boston, witch hazel blooms with tiny yellow flowers in February for those who are

A Winter Wind Break Garden Planned for a Long Season of Bloom

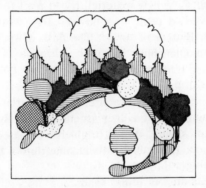

SEASON OF BLOOM OR INTEREST

WINTER — pines, yellow branches
of willow, green ground cover

APRIL — forsythia, amalanchier,
early azalea

MAY — azalea, rhododendron,
crabapple, dogwood, bulbs

JUNE — kousa dogwood, roses,
perennial flower border

JULY
AUGUST — summer annuals, potentilla,
perennials, rose of
sharon, hydrangea, silk tree

FALL — colored foliage of maple,
oak, willow, dogwood

aware enough to look. There are summer-blooming trees and shrubs. *Albizia julibrisson rosea* (silk tree) has pink feathery flowers in July, when *Stewartia* shows its camelia-like flowers. *Franklinia* blooms with three-inch white flowers in September. Between the two, *sophora japonica*, a most useful tree, bears masses of small whitish blooms in August. The Kousa dogwood tree blooms spectacularly and for a long period in late June, its white blossoms upturned to the sun (see Sequence of Bloom Chart, Chapter 15).

Fruit provides additional interest and beauty, as does fall color. Each has a charm of its own and should be counted as part of the total landscape. Bare branches and the shape of evergreens are part of the winter landscape.

When you plant new material, try to plan for a sequence of bloom. Some should come into flower early, when any blossom is a welcome harbinger of spring. The flush of spring begins with forsythia and amalanchier; it tumbles through June, each week bringing another burst of bloom and another color. Fall is the time for brilliant foliage. It begins with the early flame-colored maples, and ends with yellow birches and scarlet oaks a month later. The pure gold of quaking aspens on the Rocky Mountain slopes is breath-taking. Fruit brightens the trees and shrubs throughout the year, but is most welcome during fall and winter, when it provides food for the birds.

The well-designed home landscape uses all the valuable qualities of many plants for a garden of ever-changing beauty and excitement. A garden where something happens each month, is more interesting than a feast-or-famine yard.

13

PRIORITIES: WHAT TO BUY FIRST

THE EXISTING HOUSE

When you're faced with the prospect of paying for more plants and improvements than you can afford all at once, the question arises of where to begin and how to assign priorities. The plants needed for basic design and for positive energy saving should be planted first. Trees take precedence. Hedge material, screen, or windbreaks should be second. Usually people don't want to wait too long to renovate the front of the house—it's a matter of pride.

NEATNESS COUNTS

Overall cleanup should be done very early. Neatness covers many deficiencies in design and plant material. At first, when money is tight, a neat lawn, regularly mowed, with a crisp-cut edge, will compensate for a multitude of sins. The grass does not need to be perfect or lush or weed-free. If it's just neat it will look nice.

Future shrub borders, planted with ground cover, bulbs, even annuals, or spread with pine needles or wood chips, will give a good appearance for small cost. The front of the house may be treated this way at the beginning.

TREES

The most important plants in any landscape are the trees. They take the most time to reach an effective size. To save landscaping money, smaller trees can be bought. If they are carefully planted, watered, and fertilized in early spring, they can add several feet of growth each year. In two or three years, they will be larger than the bigger ones you could afford to buy later. Placement of trees is most important, so the total landscape plan should be completely worked out before any haphazard planting is done.

HEDGES

Hedge, screen, and windbreak material should come next. This is a good time to put up fences and walls too. If there is to be a future patio or paved walks, it's useful to have the sand base put in at this time. The paving stones can be laid later, often as a do-it-yourself job. But digging and leveling ground and spreading a truckload of sand is hard work.

Where quick growth is wanted, don't skimp on soil preparation. Nothing repays as well as a good, deep hole, enriched with old manure (peat moss, leaf-mulch, or compost will do). There is no substitute for good soil!

Growth can also be speeded up by regular fertilizing in very early spring, and plenty of water. Plants that suffer from any stress because of too little water stop growing. They start again when moistened, but the lost time is never made up. When fast growth is what you seek, buying varieties or clones known to grow fast is well worthwhile (see Plants for Hedges and Windbreaks, also Fast-Growing Trees, Chapter 15).

Most hedge plants come as tall, skinny, rooted cuttings. If they are allowed to grow without pruning, they will grow upright and always be sparse at the bottom. There are times when this pattern is desirable. For instance, a double- or triple-depth row windbreak may be wanted (tough deciduous shrubs or trees on the outside, evergreens next, and flowering material on the inside). In such a case, it is advantageous for the shrubs on the outside to grow as tall as possible as quickly as possible, and so they should be sheared as little as possible. Windbreaks and hedges should be planted fairly close together to encourage tall growth and provide an impervious screen at the top (recommended distances are in the lists of hedge and windbreak material, Chapter 15).

If you want a thick hedge, however, the young plants must be specially pruned to make them branch thickly from the bottom up. Obvious, it takes longer for them to reach the desired height. But once a hedge gets both tall and spindly on the bottom, it is a very tricky horticultural job to thicken it up. It may involve cutting the whole thing back to one or two feet high and starting over again.

It's far better to do the correct shearing for the first two years to develop the needed thick mass of twigs. Eventually, the hedge will reach the same height as it would have if you'd left it unsheared.

THE FRONT YARD

The front always seems more important that it should be. If it's neat and attractive with ground cover, woodchips, and a few flowers, it will not be an eyesore or an embarrassment. It is better to spend limited available funds on trees and energy-saving first.

How to Shear and Prune for a Thick Hedge from Young Plants

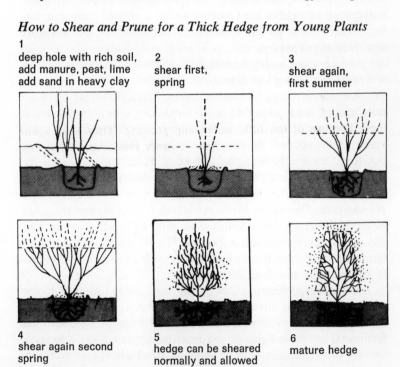

1
deep hole with rich soil, add manure, peat, lime add sand in heavy clay

2
shear first, spring

3
shear again, first summer

4
shear again second spring

5
hedge can be sheared normally and allowed to grow tall

6
mature hedge

Ground Cover and a Dogwood Tree

Sometimes a neighbor or a relative makes a critical comment, and there can be a compulsion to fix up the front for the unknown strangers who pass by.

As always, the trees come first. Consider magnolias or dogwoods at the corners of the house. Perhaps a weeping cherry or two are needed to define the entrance. Small flowering trees are excellent for use near buildings, although they should be planted at least six to eight feet from the foundation. As they grow, they will easily fill the space. Columnal trees may be planted a little closer, but even they will have a good spread at maturity.

Buying flowering trees can be tricky. Many plants are grown in Southern nurseries, even though they may be cold-hardy Northern varieties. One of the problems is that while the trees will grow in the North, their blossoms may be genetically sensitive to cold. This is especially true of dogwoods. If you are buying flowering trees, try to get them from a local nursery where they have bloomed in your area after at least one winter.

Another problem is that young trees often will not bloom until they feel old enough—a relative term. It depends on how the tree reads its microenvironment. Hard pruning, high nitrogen fertilizers, too little light, or too much water can delay flowering. On the other hand, a side dressing of super-phosphate fertilizer, minor root pruning, and a little (but not too much) drought can often stimulate flower-bud set.

There are arboriculture tricks that can help. Both depend on a plant's response to a high carbohydrate-sugar level in the branches, to encourage flower buds as opposed to leaf buds. The first trick is to tie down the branches so the ends are low, below the main part of the branch. This is done just after the normal flowering season, and left for about six weeks. The food manufactured by the leaves, instead of going to be stored in the roots, stays longer in the branches. Another trick to encourage the sugar to remain for flower bud formation is to make two or three small parallel slashes sidewise across the bottom of a few branches with a sharp, very clean, knife. Be sure the knife is free of fungus spores. Or tie a string tightly around the branch for about six weeks. (*Caution:* don't forget to take it off, or the branch will strangle and die.)

Dogwoods are particularly difficult to get blooming. Once they start, however, there is no more trouble. When you're buying flowering trees, it's worth getting ones that have already set some flower buds in the nursery.

FOUNDATION SHRUBS

When the trees are small, they will look like tall bushes. Small choice shrubs can be added as funds become available. Choose them carefully for bloom sequence, color, and eventual height.

There are two common mistakes. One is not choosing azaleas and rhododendrons in bloom. The colors can be beautiful or terrible. A cerise, an orange, and a lavender just don't make it together.

The other mistake is to buy shrubs that normally grow more than three to six feet tall at maturity. It breaks your heart to chop off the top of a healthy rhododendron, juniper or yew, because it's blocking the windows. And such a shrub can also break your back because of the pruning it requires every year. For foundation planting, use varieties that will stay low and will be the correct size at maturity (see list of Best Low-growing Shrubs for Foundation Planting, Chapter 15).

Think carefully before adding a row of little round and pointed bushes for the foundation planting. It will be a boring, costly green mustache across the front of the building. Rhododendrons and foundation evergreens are among the most expensive plants to buy. A neat foundation planting of ground cover, bulbs, annuals, a few well-chosen shrubs, and a small flowering tree or two will give a pleasant and finished look at much less cost.

ROCKS

The currently fashionable practice of planting the entire front yard with small, varied bushes in a sea of wood chips and ugly rocks is to be deplored. This idea, badly borrowed from Japanese landscape design, looks like green measles. It is possible to have shrubs, rocks, ground cover, and wood chips covering large areas, but the effect must be carefully designed. The rocks are important. To understand a rock's shape, character, and placement is very tricky. It is a most esoteric art form. Just a casual scattering of rocks and shrubs will look like the remains of a glacier on the front yard.

One of the most durable and satisfying parts of the landscape is stone. It has heat-holding qualities that can be used. However, all rocks or stone walls should look as though they really belong there. The rocks should be buried about half their height to look settled and sturdy. The most pleasing face should be visible. Rocks have movement like sculpture. Tall rocks carry the eye up. Flat ones are more restful. The Japanese, before they set a rock, spend a great deal of time looking at it. If you do that too, you can create great beauty with leftovers from building and excavating.

In nature, plant material grows near rocks because of the shelter given to their roots. If you plant, naturally, around rocks and stone walls, the effect will be successful.

GROUND COVER

Overplanting is very easy when you buy small plants. Check the mature spread and allow enough space between plants for them to grow freely. Green ground cover will pull them all together visually while they are small. Evergreen ivy, mrytle, and pachysandra are the most satisfactory plants for this purpose. Deciduous ones like violets, strawberries, and thyme are not nearly as neat, and not green during the winter.

When buying ground cover plants, you'll find several sizes and prices available. The cheapest are just rooted cuttings, generally sold in large flat wooden boxes of 100 plants. Planted in good soil and watered, they will grow fast. The next larger size is small individual plants in small pots costing from 50¢ to $1. Larger sizes with stronger root systems are available in larger pots.

Ground covers may be easily moved from one place on your lot to another in early spring. Given good care, they will root easily. Such plants take longer to become established than bought plants, but they'll eventually look just the same. The least expensive plants are those grown by a friend. Usually they are from good sturdy stock or your friend wouldn't have extra. Wash them carefully to avoid bringing in insects or disease.

However, if you pay someone to do the planting, it is more economical to buy flats of plants. Making cuttings from existing plants is too time-consuming.

All ground covers need a well-prepared bed. The evergreens need a soft, organic soil (mix one-third volume of peat moss). The peat moss doesn't need to be worked in very deeply, only in the top six inches. Ivy, myrtle, and pachysandra prefer some shade, but pachysandra will stand more sun than the others. However, in hot, full sun, use creeping euonymus, sedum, or thyme, creeping fig in Southern areas. Do not plant ivy near new concrete.

How to Root Ground Covers from Existing Plants

Nip off growing tips to one or two pairs of leaves. Leave green leaves above ground. Twist long stems into circle. Bury roots and keep moist until plants begin to grow and put out new leaves.

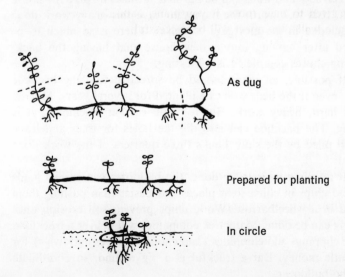

As dug

Prepared for planting

In circle

The ground is too alkaline from the lime or calcium used in concrete.

All ground-cover plants must be faithfully sprinkled until the roots become established, usually for about a year. A mulch helps, but don't use grass clippings, or anything that will introduce weed seeds. The closer the plants are spaced, the sooner they will give the desired effect.

THE IMPORTANCE OF A PLAN

Buying plants is expensive. Renovating is expensive. Moving plants around is difficult. Anybody hates to do it all twice or three times because it doesn't look good at first.

Calculate the landscape needs for both energy saving and esthetics. Don't overlook privacy, usability, and ease of maintenance.

THE NEW HOUSE: BUYING PRIORITIES

For a new house, a total plan is essential for most economical use of landscape dollars. If the plan is done before building begins, many valuable trees and shrubs can be protected or moved. Also, loam can be stockpiled where it will be needed.

Terraces and walls can be finished at the same time the house is built. It is well worth the money to have this heavy work done and included in the mortgage expenses. There is so much to be finished after moving into a new house that having the back-breaking chores completed is a blessing.

If possible, all loam should be spread before the backhoe leaves, even if the beds won't be planted for several years. Moving soil is hard, heavy work. But for construction machinery, it is nothing. The backhoe can also dig the holes for trees and leave the soil piled by the side. That's three quarters of the work done for you.

If no planting is to be done, the bulldozer can spread loads of wood chips in convenient places. It's easier than pushing them around in a wheelbarrow. Wood chips prevent soil erosion until planting can be done. Many tree companies will deliver a truckload of tree clippings and chippings (and chopped leaves and twigs) for very little money. But a truckful is a big mound, so coordinate with the bulldozer.

PROTECTING EXISTING TREES DURING CONSTRUCTION

If you are fortunate enough to acquire your lot before the bulldozer has leveled it, there will probably be trees on the property. They may look very small. Price their equivalents before you heed the builder's, "Oh, you can get another weed tree like that." You may even be fortunate enough to have a good large specimen or a grove.

Protecting trees during construction is simple if you understand their growth requirements. Smaller trees have small root areas through which they live. Large ones can have enormous circles that nourish them. Trees breathe and drink through these roots. Protect these areas with fencing or markers and rope.

Contractors can't be bothered protecting trees—it takes time, and time is money. You need to be aware that the soil as far from the trunk as the outer edge of the leaves (the "drip line") should not be disturbed or packed down. That means: no vehicle under the trees, no storage of heavy material, no cutting of the roots, no grade changes over them, and most important: NO SOIL ADDED OVER THE ROOTS. Many people buy nice wooded lots, graded and planted with grass. In a few years, the trees decline and die. The roots were simply smothered with topsoil. The rules are simple:

> Never add more than three to six inches of anything over the roots.
> Don't compress the soil.
> Don't throw waste paint or light fires over the roots.
> Don't cut more than one third of the total root run.

Sometimes a building must be constructed close to an existing tree. It can be very close, even within only several feet. A tree can tolerate losing up to one third of that circle of roots under the drip line. The remaining two thirds needs protection. After construction is finished, cut away about one third of the branches and limbs. The tree will better stand root damage, and it will be a safer tree.

If you must raise or lower the grade (ground level), use retaining walls. To raise the grade directly over the soil, first add crushed stone, leaving vents to the surface for air. Next add perforated black plastic. Then add the soil. Drainage tiles may be necessary for additional aeration. It is expensive to raise the grade over an existing tree. Consider a deck instead. It will give you the same outdoor living space. The roots will be fine underneath, with no fancy treatment.

Existing wild shrubs on a building lot are generally not worth the time they take to move. Any good ones can be dropped on the property border by the bulldozer and left to grow. But protect any outlying area that has forest-type undergrowth. Stepped on once too often, it does not grow back.

14

MAINTENANCE
AND COMMON SENSE

LAWNS

A lawn is a high-maintenance item. It can be maintained as a beautiful, green carpet by weekly mowing, two or three fertilizings each year, weed killer, fungicide, insecticide, the seeding of bare spots, and regular watering. If money is no object, it's easy to hire people to handle the chores, albeit at very generous pay. For the less-discriminating, it's handy to remember that almost every red-blooded American boy knows how to mow a lawn, and one of them is always looking for work. The minimum maintenance for a lawn is mowing about every ten days to a height of two inches. For a better lawn, fertilizing once a year, liming every three years, and watering during dry spells is necessary. A magnificent lawn requires considerably more care. In fact, it's a labor of love, almost to becoming an obsession. You can't have one without the other.

There are rough lawns. A meadow is easy to grow. However, it's hard to find anyone who will mow it once or twice a year when the grass is high. A conservation meadow is mowed first in July after the ground-nesting birds are gone. A lawn in the shade needs only occasional mowing, but it has a sparse, woodsy look. Most fastidious homeowners won't find it neat enough.

Grass is a cool-weather plant. It grows best in spring and fall. If you're content with grass that's less than a green carpet, you

117

can have an ordinary lawn by providing only reasonable care. Save all grass clippings in a mulch pile. In a year or two, it will turn into good compost, which can be used in place of bought peat moss or topsoil—another saving of dollars.

There are special grasses for hot climates. They are rough-textured and usually can't be grown from seed. They brown out if not watered. They need less mowing than grass in cool climates. Lawns in hot climates are very desirable from an energy standpoint. The cooling effect they exert around buildings outweighs the maintenance required. In hot climates, sometimes shrubs or thick ground cover provides a home for undesirable insects, pests, and snakes.

GROUND COVERS

A pleasing green carpet can be achieved with ground covers, too. They don't need constant care once they're established. They do need one annual weeding, usually during late spring. They need water during droughts, or when their leaves droop.

In arid or Northern areas, ground cover should not be raked clean. The decaying leaves underneath return nutrients to the soil. In moist tropical areas, however, the fallen leaves and debris may become rank and unattractive. An occasional light raking is beneficial. After raking, the exposed soil and roots are very susceptible to sun burn and drought, so they should be watered.

Renovation maintenance on ground covers is usually done in very early spring, when hormones that promote vigorous new growth are active. Ground covers benefit from being clipped back. New shoots then grow to thicken the beds.

SHRUBS

Shrubs are very self-sufficient. They need little care. But if they're neglected entirely, they take lots of effort to restore and renovate. When young, shrubs should be fed every year or two in spring, and watered during droughts. When mature, they need little feeding, which makes them grow more and require more pruning. As they age, shrubs become susceptible to attacks of fungi and insects. If the leaves look mottled or speckled, it could be scale, white fly, or other sucking insects. It could be fungus. It could be just hunger for some plant food. Consult your local extension service or nursery for accurate identification before spending money for a cure.

A light yearly pruning or shaping will keep shrubs looking well for many years, and keep them neat as they grow older. Eventually, many shrubs get too large or overgrown, or too sparse. Most deciduous shrubs can be cut back severely without harm. Evergreens must be pruned more conservatively. Correct renewal pruning is a skill. Each species must be done a certain way at a certain season (see Shrubs, Chapter 10).

Proper pruning is especially important for food-bearing plants. Find out before you hack away. The library is a good source of information. So is the agricultural extension service.

Don't assume your gardener or grass-cutter knows better than you do. Too many so-called "landscape gardeners" prune everything like a privet hedge. Many a valuable shrub has been ruined by a trusted gardener.

HEDGES AND OTHER SHEARED SHRUBS

These require the most work. There is no doubt that neat, clipped hedges and borders are a joy to behold. Unfortunately, they are no joy to keep neat. If left untended, they quickly look messy (slower-growing plants require less shearing less often). However, with labor costs so high, many people decide to prefer "naturalistic" hedges and shrubs. A light shearing when the spirit moves you will encourage thick growth (see Chapters 10 and 13).

Power mowers and hedge clippers have made maintenance easier, but it still takes time and gasoline.

TREES

Established trees need little regular maintenance. If their roots are near or under a lawn, they will have all the fertilizer and extra water they need. Established trees, rarely need feeding. Once every three to five years is adequate if vigorous growth is wanted. Sometimes old trees get diseases, are attacked by insects, or suffer a decline in health. In these instances, fertilizer is indicated.

Fertilizer may be sprinkled on the surface of the ground and watered in thoroughly. It is not necessary to punch holes in the ground all around the tree, as is usually recommended. Occasionally fertilizer or fungicide is administered directly into the trunk through tubing inserted in holes drilled in the bark. This job is for a professional tree company and is used only in emergencies.

All trees appreciate a good soaking of their roots during severe droughts. Mature trees have long, deep roots, often 60 feet or more. They get water from the deep, underground water table during summer and are less sensitive than younger trees are to temporary drought. City trees, however, have a more difficult time finding water. The building of roads and foundations interferes with the underground water table. When storm water is piped into a sewer, it doesn't recharge the underground streams. The more built-up an area is, the more extra summer water the tree needs.

As trees get older, they occasionally require the pruning of overgrown or dangerous branches. Again, a professional tree company should be called. Pruning large trees is expensive, but a branch through the roof is more expensive. Pruning large trees is also dangerous. Anyone who goes up a tree on your property should have liability insurance. Otherwise, if he falls, you could be sued. Make sure he carries Workmen's Compensation for his employees. A self-employed man may give you in advance a written statement relieving you of responsibility for himself, if he should have an accident.

Always ask for an estimate (or better still, a bid) before work begins. Don't be afraid to get several bids. When in doubt, use registered or certified arborists.

Young trees are a different matter. They need fertilizing every year or two to maintain a rapid growth rate. They should be pruned to improve their shape. A mature tree is only the product of its youthful shape and form (see Tree Pruning, Chapter 9).

Eventually, all trees are attacked by insects and fungi. When this problem occurs, check with your local extension forester or tree company before buying equipment and chemicals. Make sure you need a spraying company before you hire one. Every little bug is not a crisis. There is no substitute for competent professional appraisal. Money is easily wasted on the wrong spray at the wrong time. Some epidemics are self-limiting and don't permanently damage healthy trees.

In general, if something is chewing the leaves, spray with methoxychlor or sevin in the evening after the bees have gone in, and when the wind is low. If the problem is aphids, sooty mold, or any sucking insect (other than scale) use malathion or diazinon. Use only according to the directions on the package. All chemicals can be dangerous.

Any tree that has suffered insect damage will enjoy a late fall fertilizing.

DUTCH ELM DISEASE

Dutch elm disease is a special case. Because so many elms were planted decades ago and because there is still no cure, control of the disease is a problem.

Proper control depends on good sanitation—which means *immediate* removal of diseased and dying trees. It has to be a townwide effort to be effective. The disease-spreading beetles will fly for miles to find a suitable tree. The best thing a homeowner can do is have his own trees sprayed two or three times a year by the best tree company in town. The hope is that this treatment will deter the beetle from bringing the disease to his trees.

If a tree has more than 10 percent of its leaves infected, it should be removed immediately. The job is expensive, but the tree will have to be cut down eventually, anyway. It won't cost any less later. In the meantime, though, it will serve as a reservoir of infection to spread to other trees. There are fungicides (Benlate–BPL or Carbenzadim) that can be injected yearly into the trees to deter disease. They are still experimental and have not yet been a complete success.

FERTILIZERS

Not all fertilizers are the same, but the chemicals they release are. And any fertilizer is useful only if the instructions on the label are followed accurately. It is easy to burn plants with too much fertilizer salts.

Basically the three numbers on the package stand for nitrogen, phosphorous, and potash (or potassium). The classic is 5–10–5, which stands for 5 percent nitrogen, 10 percent phosphorous and 5 percent potash. All three elements are in the right proportion for good plant growth. The right proportion is essential. The percentages can be manipulated to change the growth pattern of a plant, but too much manipulation causes physiological problems.

Nitrogen mainly promotes leaf growth. Phosphorous makes strong roots and stems and promotes flowering. Potash enhances maturity and ripening of seeds and fruits. In addition phosphorous and potash give added insect and disease resistance.

Nitrogen moves quickly through the soil, and nitrogen disappears faster as the temperature rises. Phosphorous, on the other hand, moves very slowly and dissolves very slowly. It lasts longer than nitrogen.

Grass is usually fed with a high-nitrogen compound (10–6–4) to make it greener and to grow faster. Shrubs and trees generally do better with 5–10–5. Occasionally they are given more nitrogen to make them grow faster.

Fertilizers may be "man-made" chemicals which are quickly dissolved in ground water. They give a quick burst of growth for about six weeks. Or fertilizers may be "organic," made from substances that were once alive (leaves, manure, bonemeal, cottonseed, urea.) These release the same chemicals at a slow, steady rate over a long period of time. They are generally more expensive than regular chemical fertilizers.

If your plants need a quick pick-me-up, liquid fertilizers become available to the plants fastest of all, through the leaves as well as the soil.

Generally, for home landscape use, the organic fertilizers are best in the long run. They needn't be applied so often and they never burn the plants. Also, organic fertilizers improve the texture of the soil so things grow better. Chemical fertilizers are used where cost is a factor. They are made from petroleum and mineral salts, and waste energy dollars. Old manure (natural or bought in bags) is better for the plants and saves oil.

Soil science is complicated. It involves not only fertilizers but also lime, trace elements (metals such as magnesium, manganese, cobalt, and iron), and helpful fungi and insects. Most of these are of more concern to farmers. Rarely do they cause problems in the home garden. Lime is the only substance that should be tested for regularly, especially on lawns. It keeps the soil from becoming too acid, and actually improves its texture. Any good nursery will test your soil for acidity or alkalinity (called "pH") and will recommend the needed correction. However, be sure to tell the nurserymen what is to be grown in the soil. Rhododendrons, azaleas, dogwood, redbud, most evergreens, and many trees prefer a slightly acid soil. Lilacs and grass prefer it neutral.

WATERING

All plants need water. They can grow only as fast as they have water for cell growth. Trees in the rain forest grow so fast because of the available water.

One deep watering is worth a peck of sprinklings. Most plants require one inch of rainfall each week. If you turn on the sprinkler, it should fill a glass up to a depth of one inch before you turn it off. During time of drought, very hot, dry or windy weather, this should be increased to two or three times a week.

Water is a valuable resource, not to be wasted. Overwatering doesn't help plants. Excess water just percolates through the soil into the lower levels. The moving of water uses energy to bring it to your hose, whether through a municipal system or from your own electric pump. Furthermore, plants, especially trees and shrubs, can die from too much water. Roots need air or they smother and rot. A good watering that is allowed to soak through and then dry out is preferred to frequent light waterings. Only swamp plants like wet feet.

Light sprinklings don't reach the deeper roots. Sprinklings encourage the plants to put out new roots near the surface of the soil. These roots are very susceptible to drying out as the top layer of soil heats up. The lower levels remain quite constant in temperature.

Watering stimulates "soft" growth. Lack of water causes plants to "harden." Their outer covering becomes tough and leathery. Both leaves and bark are affected. Water is also a triggering mechanism by which the plants know what seasons are coming, especially in tropical regions where there is less pronounced temperature variation. When the rains come (usually spring) the plants know to begin putting out leaves and flowers. When the rains diminish (usually in the fall), the plants begin to "harden" to conserve moisture and protect their cells from winter cold to come. Home watering should mimic the seasons. It is wise to water more often in May and June when it is dry, than in September and October. However, all plants should go into winter with moisture in the soil. One good soaking in fall is desirable if the weather has been unseasonably dry.

A good general rule to decide if watering is needed is: if the soil is dry six inches down, or if there has not been a good rainfall recently that soaked in and did not run off.

PART
III

CHAPTER

15

PLANT LISTS FOR SPECIAL PURPOSES

TREES

1. Trees of Different Heights—Small, Medium, Large
2. Columnar Trees
3. Trees with a Wide Range of Climate Adaptability—Vigorous and Reliable
4. Fast-growing Trees
5. Trees that Grow in the Shade—Understory Planting
6. Trees for Cities, Useful for Sidewalks, Courtyards, and Paved Areas
7. Trees that are Hard to Transplant

SHRUBS

8. Commonly Used Deciduous Shrubs
9. Commonly Used Evergreen Shrubs
10. Low-growing Shrubs for Foundation Planting
11. Shrubs that Grow in the Shade—Understory Planting

GROUND COVERS

12. Best Ground Covers for Sun
13. Best Ground Covers for Shade
14. Fast-growing Vines for Trellises and Fences
15. Evergreen Vines for the South

PLANTS FOR SPECIAL SITUATIONS

16. Windbreak Plants for the Great Plains—Shelterbelts
17. Windbreaks for Normal Soil
18. Drought-resistant Plants for Desert and Dry Areas
19. Sequence of Bloom
20. Growth-rate Comparison of Selected Trees
21. Pollution Sensitivity

Plant List 1

TREES OF DIFFERENT HEIGHTS AT MATURITY

LARGE TREES (over 50')	Size	Rate of Growth	Zone	Description
Abies concolor White fir	100'+	moderate	4–9	*evergreen; bluish needles
Acer platanoides Norway maple	90'	moderate	3–9	gives dense shade; reliable; yellow fall color
Acer rubrum Red maple	100'	fast	3–9	good fall color; moist soil
Acer sacchrum Sugar maple	100'+	moderate	3–8	good fall color; salt sensitive; not for cities; sap gives maple sugar
Acer saccharinum Silver or cut-leaf maple	80'	very fast	3–8	not near pipes or buildings; weak-wooded
Aesculus carnea Red horse chestnut	75'	slow	3–6 and Calif.	pink flowers; horse chestnuts
Aesculus hippocastanum "Baumanni" Baumann horse chestnut	75'	slow	3–6	white flowers; no nuts; no summer drought
Ailanthus altissima Tree of heaven	60'	very fast	4–9	grows anywhere; female tree only; weedy tree; from *A Tree Grows in Brooklyn*
Araucaria varieties Norfolk pine, Monkey puzzle, Bunya-bunya	90'	moderate	10	*evergreen; unusual shapes

* Evergreen.

LARGE TREES (over 50')	Size	Rate of Growth	Zone	Description
†*Betula papyrifera* Canoe birch	90'	moderate	2–4	needs cold winters; beautiful white bark; good foliage; hard to move
†*Betula nigra* Black birch	80'	moderate	4–9	short lived in North; wet locations
Carpinus betulus European hornbeam	60'	slow	5–9	many shapes available; can be sheared
Casuarina equisetifolia She-oak, Horsetail, Beefwood	70'	fast	9–10	salt and wind resistant; tolerates sand *evergreen; crowds other trees
Catalpa speciosa Northern catalpa	90'	moderate	4–7	large, coarse tree; flowers; stands drought and heat
Cedrus atlantica Atlas cedar	100'+	slow	6–10	*evergreen; silvery color
Cedrus libani Cedar of Lebanon	80'	slow	5–10	*evergreen; wide-spreading when old
Celtis australis European hackberry	50–75'	moderate	6–10	withstands drought
†*Cercidiphyllum japonicum* Katsura tree	60'	moderate	4–8	wide-spreading tree; pest free; hard to move; attractive leaves
Chamaecyparis obtusa Hinoki false cypress	100'+	slow	4–8	*evergreen; moist air
Cocos nucifera Coconut palm	80'	slow	10	Florida palm tree; slow starting; subject to new diseases

†*Cornus nuttalli* Pacific dogwood	75'	moderate	7–9	*evergreen; most beautiful tree; flowers; moist air; West Coast tree
Corylus colurna Turkish filbert	75'	moderate	4–8	tolerates dry soil; nice shape
Cryptomeria japonica Cryptomeria	100'+	moderate	5–8	*evergreen; attractive; soft foliage
Cupressus macrocarpa Monterey cypress	75'	fast	7–9	*evergreen; withstands salt spray and wind; old trees develop interesting shapes
Eucalyptus varieties Red, white, or silver-dollar gum tree	100'+	fastest	9–10	big, tall trees; Do not use blue gum variety, except for rural reforestation
†*Fagus sylvatica* European beech	90'	slow	4–8	beautiful tree; wide, low, shallow roots; moist soil
Fraxinus pennsylvanica 'Marshall's Seedless' Marshall seedless ash (green ash)	60'	fast	3–9	good shade tree; seedless variety
†*Gingko biloba* gingko	to 100'	slow	4–10	each clone has a different shape; slow starting; use only male trees; pest free
Gleditsia triacanthos inermis Thornless honey locust (see illustration 47, Chapter 12) Moraine, Majestic, Skyline, Shademaster	70'	fast	4–10	light shade; lawn will grow under it; city- and drought-tolerant; reliable; different clones have different shapes; leafs out late in spring; drops leaves early in fall
†*Liquidambar styraciflua* Sweet gum	100'	moderate	5–10	attractive shade tree; good fall color

† Spring planting only, hard to move.

LARGE TREES (over 50')	Size	Rate of Growth	Zone	Description
†*Liriodendron tulipfera* Tulip tree	100'	fast	4–9	grows broad and large; green flowers
Magnolia grandiflora Southern magnolia	90'	moderate	7–9	*evergreen; big flowers; attractive tree in South; shrubby in North
Metasequoia glyptostroboides Dawn redwood (recently brought from China)	100'	fast	5–9	deciduous needles; bright green; attractive, upright shape
†*Nyssa sylvatica* Tupelo or black gum	90'	slow	4–9	swampy places; good fall color
Picea varieties Spruce	75–100'	moderate	2–5	*evergreen; many useful varieties; good at high altitudes
Pinus varieties Pine	50–100'	fast	2–10	*evergreen; useful for dry soils
Pittosporum rhombifolium Diamond leaf pittosporum	80'	moderate	10	*evergreen
Platanus acerifolia "Bloodgood" Bloodgood London plane	100'	fast	5–9	large tree; good in city; "Bloodgood" clone is anthracnose fungus resistant
Podocarpus macrophyllus Yew podocarpus	60'	slow	7–10	*evergreen; good green; can be clipped
†*Prunus sargenti* Sargent cherry	75'	moderate	4–8	flowers; fall color; beautiful tree
Pseudolarix amabilis Golden larch	100'	moderate	5–8	deciduous; needles; yellow fall color

	Size	Rate of Growth	Zone	Description
Pseudotsuga menziesii Douglas-fir	200'	fast	4–6	*evergreen; attractive; Pacific coast
†*Quercus* varieties Oak	60–100'	slow	3–10	good, large shade tree; sturdy once established; gets insects and fungi but still most useful
†*Sophora japonica* Japanese pagoda tree	75'	moderate	4–8	lovely tree; flowers; good in city; insect free
Taxodium distichum Bald cypress	150'	moderate	4–10	deciduous; needles; swamps and wet places
Thuja occidentalis American arborvitae	60'	moderate	2–5	*evergreen; grows anywhere; columnar; not the most beautiful, but reliable
Tilia cordata Little leaf linden, European linden	90'	moderate	3–8	good, neat tree; good in city
Tilia varieties American linden, Silver linden	75–100'	moderate	2–8	larger leaves; good, useful trees; fragrant when in bloom
Tsuga canadensis Canadian hemlock	90'	moderate	3–6	*evergreen; most graceful tree in sheltered spot; good foliage
Zelkova serrata "Village Green" Village Green zelkova	90'	moderate	5–10	excellent tree; wide-spreading; low spreading unless pruned up

†Spring planting only, hard to move.

MEDIUM-SIZE TREES (30' to 50')	Size	Rate of Growth	Zone	Description
Acacia decurrens Silver wattle	50'	fast	9–10	good soil; short-lived; flowers; *evergreen

MEDIUM-SIZE TREES (30' to 50')	Size	Rate of Growth	Zone	Description
Acer platanoides "Crimson King" Crimson King Norway maple	50'	slow	4–8	red leaves all summer and fall
Aesculus glabra Yellow buckeye	35'	moderate	3–7	flowers; good fall color; horse chestnuts
Albizia julibrisson rosea Silk tree	40'	fast	5–10	pink flowers in summer; dainty leaf; attractive, spreading tree; feathery
Amelanchier canadensis Shadblow serviceberry	50'	moderate	4–8	grows in shade; very early spring blooms (blooms when the shad run)
Amelanchier, varieties Serviceberry, Saskatoon	40'	moderate–fast	3–8	varieties for each area of country; flowers
†*Betula pendula (verrucosa)* European weeping birch	50'	fast	2–8	lovely tree; white bark; short-lived; gets borers and leaf miners
Camellia japonica Common camellia	40'	slow	7–9	beautiful blooms and foliage; acid soil; *evergreen; cool nights
Cassia fistula Golden shower, senna	35'	moderate	10	beautiful yellow blooms
Circus canadensis Redbud	35'	moderate	4–8	delicate pink flowers; grows in shade
Cladrastis lutea American yellow-wood	50'	moderate	4–8	nice tree; flowers; stands heat and cold
Delonix regia Royal poinciana	40'	moderate	10	outstanding scarlet blooms; spreading

Eucalyptus ficifolia Red flowering gum	50'	fast	10	vigorous tree; shallow roots steal food from surrounding plants; flowers
Fraxinus velutina Modesto ash	50'	fast	5–10	grows in dry alkaline soil; especially California and West
Gleditsia triacanthos inermis "Sunburst" Sunburst honey locust	40'	fast	4–10	new leaves bright yellow; grows in any soil
Jacaranda acutifolia Jacaranda	50'	moderate	10	blue flowers early in spring; Florida and California
Juniperus scopulorum Rocky mountain juniper	35'	slow	4–8	*evergreen; drought-tolerant; used west of Illinois
†*Koelreuteria paniculata* Golden rain tree	35'	moderate	5–10	yellow flowers; irregular shape; drought-resistant; reliable, hard to move
†*Magnolia loebneri* "Merrill" Merrill magnolia	50'	moderate	4–8	white flowers, excellent large magnolia for Northern areas
†*Magnolia virginiana* Sweet bay	10–60'	slow	5–9	shrub in North, tree in South; moist soil; *evergreen
Malus baccata Siberian crabapple	50'	moderate	2–7	flowers; small fruit; upright
Melia azedarach China berry	45'	fast	7–10	stands heat and drought; lilac flowers; reliable
†*Phellodendron amurense* Amur cork tree	35'	fast	3–6	low branching; good in city; insect free
†*Pyrus calleryana* "Bradford" Bradford callery pear	40'	moderate	5–10	good city tree; small flowers; neat shape; good fall color

MEDIUM-SIZE TREES (30' to 50')	Size	Rate of Growth	Zone	Description
Sapium sebiferum Chinese tallow tree	40'	moderate	9–10	good in South; reliable
Schinus terebinthifolius Brazil pepper tree	40'	moderate	9–10	stands dry soil
Sorbus acuparia European mountain ash	45'	fast	3–6	flowers; good bright berries in sun; upright; neat; gets borers
Tilia cordata "Greenspire" Greenspire little leaf linden	45'	moderate	3–9	upright; oval crown; neat tree; transplants easily; good in city

†Spring planting only, hard to move.

SMALL TREES (under 30')	Size	Rate of Growth	Zone	Description
Acer circinatum Vine maple	25'	slow	5–7	partial shade; West Coast tree
Acer ginnala Amur maple	20'	slow	2–7	hardy; no-care; good screen; beautiful fall color
†*Acer palmatum* Japanese maple (red and green leaves)	20'	slow	5–8	choice tree; delicate foliage; good fall color; some red-leaved varieties turn green in summer; best ones stay red
Acer tataricum Tatarian maple	30'	slow	3–7	hardy; no-care; good screen
Amelanchier grandiflora Apple serviceberry	25'	moderate	4–7	early flowers; grows in shade

Name	Height	Growth	Zone	Notes
Bauhinia blakeana Orchid tree	30'	moderate	10	beautiful flowers; long blooming
Chionanthus virginicus Fringe tree	30'	moderate	4–9	feathery flowers; late leafing; attractive; fruit
†*Cornus florida* Flowering dogwood	30'	moderate	5–9	most beautiful tree; acid soil; sun or shade; lovely flowers
†*Cornus kousa* Kousa or Korean dogwood	25'	moderate	5–9	late flowering; beautiful; sun
Crataegus lavallei Lavalle hawthorne	20'	moderate	4–7	flowers; thorns; fruits
Crataegus phaenopyrum Washington hawthorne	30'	moderate	4–7	dry or alkaline soil; stands wind; flowers; fruits
Elaeagnus angustifolia Russian olive	20'	fast	2–10	silver leaves; grows anywhere; good screen
Ficus carica Common fig	30'	moderate	6–10	coarse leaves; spreading
†*Franklinia alatamaha* Franklinia	25'	moderate	5–9	fine flowers and fall color; protect in North from cold in spring
Ilex vomitoria Yaupon	25'	moderate	7–9	*evergreen; hedge or tree; may be sheared
†*Lagerstroemia indica* Crape-myrtle	25'	moderate–fast	7–9	good flowers; hard to move; plant small size
Laurus nobilis Laurel or bay tree (used in ancient Greece)	30'	slow	6–9	*evergreen; hedge or tree; shears well

SMALL TREES (under 30')	Size	Rate of Growth	Zone	Description
Ligustrum lucidum Glossy privet	30'	fast	7–10	*evergreen; hedge or tree; shears well; reliable; vigorous
†*Magnolia soulangana* Saucer magnolia	25'	moderate	5–8	beautiful early bloom; hard to move; good in city
Malus varieties crabapple	10–30'	moderate	2–8	beautiful blooms; fruit, very reliable; useful
Myrica californica California bayberry	30'	moderate	7–10	*evergreen; shrub or tree
Olea europaea Common olive	25'	very slow	9–10	dry climate; long-lived, spreading; fruit; *evergreen
†*Prunus* varieties Cherry	15–30'	moderate	5–8 (some 2–7)	lovely flowers; some with edible fruit
Syringa amurensis japonica Japanese tree lilac	30'	moderate	3–8	good flowers late in season; reliable; watch for scale and borer
Viburnum sieboldii Siebold viburnum	30'	moderate	4–8	shrub or tree; flowers; fruit; vigorous

Plant List 2

COLUMNAR, UPRIGHT GROWING TREES

(For shade from the summer sun, narrow courtyards and streets). Note: Also called "fastigate" or "sentry." Always buy a named clone.

	Size	Rate of Growth	Zone	Description
Acer platanoides "Columnare" Columnar Norway maple	50'	moderate	3	transplants easily
Acer rubrum "Columnare" Columnar red maple	75'	fast	3	good fall color; moist soil
Acer saccharum "Columnare," "Newton Sentry," or "Monumentale" Columnar sugar maple	60'	moderate	3	good fall color; very narrow
†*Fagus sylvatica fastigata* Upright European beech	50'	slow	4	beautiful tree; long-lived
†*Gingko biloba* "Fastigata" or "Sentry" Sentry gingko	60'	moderate	4	moist soil at first; pollution-resistant; very narrow; beautiful tree; good in city
Malus "Van Eseltine" Upright Van Eseltine crabapple	20'	fast	4	beautiful flowers; low branches
Populus alba pyramidalis Bolleana poplar	50'	fast	3	less susceptible to canker disease; caution—roots get in water and sewer pipes

†Spring planting only, hard to move.

	Size	Rate of Growth	Zone	Description
Populus nigra italica Lombardy poplar	80'	fastest	3	narrow; VERY susceptible to canker disease; caution—roots get in water and sewer pipes
Prunus sargenti "Columnaris" Upright sargent cherry	45'	slow	4	beautiful flowers; nice tree; hard to find
Prunus serrula "Amanogawa" Amanogawa Japanese cherry	20'	slow	6	beautiful flowers; nice tree
Quercus robur fastigiata Pyramidal English oak	75'	slow	5	beautiful tree; long-lived
Ulmus hollandica Groenveldt Groenveldt elm	90'	moderate	4	semiresistant to Dutch elm disease; upright, but wider than the other trees on list

Plant List 3

TREES WITH A WIDE RANGE OF CLIMATE ADAPTABILITY, VIGOROUS AND RELIABLE

	Size	Rate of Growth	Zone	Description
Albizia julibrisson rosea Silk tree	40'	fast	5–10	pink flowers; mimosa-type leaves; graceful, spreading shape
Calocedrus decurrens California incense cedar	90'	slow	6–10	*evergreen; moist climate; upright

Name	Height	Growth	Zones	Notes
Cedrus libani Cedar of Lebanon	80'	slow	5–10	*evergreen; spreading when old
Celtis australis European hackberry	50–75'	moderate	6–10	withstands drought; elm-like leaves; not choice, but useful
Elaeagnus angustifolia Russian olive	20'	fast	2–10	silvery leaves; grows anywhere; salt and wind resistant; good screen
Fraxinus pennsylvanica "Marshall's Seedless" Marshall seedless ash (green ash)	60'	fast	3–9	good shade tree; seedless
Fraxinus velutina Modesto ash	50'	fast	5–10	grows in dry, alkaline soil, especially West and California
Gleditsia triacanthos inermis Thornless honey locust	35–70'	fast	4–10	reliable street tree; light shade; grass will grow under it; not graceful in winter
Juniperus chinensis varieties Chinese juniper	to 30'	moderate	5–10	*evergreen, useful
Malus varieties Crabapple	10–50'	moderate	2–8	beautiful spring flowers; fruit
Pyrus calleryana "Bradford" Bradford callery pear	40'	moderate	5–10	pollution-resistant; white flowers; leathery leaves; good in city
Zelkova serrata "Village Green" Village Green zelkova	60'	fast	5–10	good shape; good shade tree; withstands wind, drought, and alkaline soil

*Evergreen

Plant List 4

FAST-GROWING TREES

Good for windbreaks and screens; too vigorous to grow near buildings; should be planted at edge of property or 60 feet from buildings.

	Size	Rate of Growth	Hardy to Zone	Description
Casaurina equisetifolia She-oak, Horsetail, Beefwood	70'	fast	9–10	*evergreen; shallow-rooted; stands sand, wind, drought, and salt water
Eucalyptus globulus Blue gum	200'	fastest	9–10	*evergreen; coarse tree; drops litter; reliable but large
Grevillea robusta Silk-oak	150'	fast	10	*evergreen; attractive; shallow roots
Phyllostachys bambusoides Japanese timber bamboo	70'	fast	7–10	*evergreen; very invasive; spreads everywhere by underground roots
Populus varieties Poplar, Cottonwood	50–100'	fast	1–9	attractive tree but roots go into pipes; drops litter
Populus nigra italica Lombardy poplar	90'	fast	3–8	beautiful; narrow and tall; gets canker just as it reaches maturity
Populus tremuloides Quaking aspen	90'	fast	1–7	picturesque; plant in groves; good fall color
Salix varieties Willow	50–75'	fast	2–10	beautiful, graceful tree; roots get in water pipes; drops litter
Ulmus varieties Elm	50–120'	fast	2–10	superb tree but gets incurable disease

*Evergreen

Plant List 5

Useful for understory planting.

TREES THAT GROW IN SHADE

	Size	Rate of Growth	Zone	Description
Acer circinatum Vine maple	25'	slow	5–8	twining trunk; good fall color; West Coast
Acer pennsylvanicum Striped maple	35'	moderate	3–7	striped bark
Amelanchier varieties Serviceberry	30'	moderate	3–7	flowers very early; berries; shrubby
Cercis canadensis Redbud	35'	fast	4–9	acid soil; lovely pink flowers
Cornus florida Dogwood	40'	moderate	5–9	most beautiful tree; flowers; acid soil
Ilex varieties Holly	6–50'	slow	5–8	dark foliage; acid soil; some evergreen
Magnolia virginiana Sweet bay	10–60'	slow	5–9	*evergreen; white flowers; tall in South; shrubby in North and not evergreen
Podocarpus varieties podocarpus	60'	moderate	7–10	*evergreen; attractive, yew-like foliage
Prunus pennsylvanica Pin cherry	30'	fast	2–6	flowers; berries; sparse habit of growth

*Evergreen

	Size	Rate of Growth	Zone	Description
Thuja occidentalis American arborvitae	50'	fast	2–6	*evergreen; columnar tree; grows in any soil
Tsuga varieties Hemlock	75–200'	moderate	3–7	*evergreen; good soil; moisture; beautiful tree; can be sheared

Plant List 6

TREES FOR CITIES

Useful for sidewalks, courtyards, paved areas. Clones developed especially for or suited to city streets.

	Size	Rate of Growth	Hardy to Zone	Description
THE MAPLES *Acer platanoides*, Norway maple				all varieties transplant easily, yellow fall color
Emerald Queen	60'	rapid	3	upright; oval head
Cleveland	50'	slower	3	upright; oval head
Summershade	60'	rapid	3	broad shape; resistant to leaf scorch; good central leader and straight trunk
Greenlace	50'	slower	3	cut leaf; upright growth
Crimson King	40'	slow	4	wine-red leaves, all season
Acer rubrum, Red maple				all varieties require more water than Norway maples, all varieties grow faster than Norway maples, red fall color

Name	Height	Rate	Zone	Notes
Armstrong	35'	rapid	3	narrow
Autumn Flame	60'	moderate	3	small leaves; colors and defoliates early
Gerling	35'	moderate	3	similar to Armstrong; wider shape
October Glory	50'	rapid	3	good green leaves; glossy; globe-shaped; good fall color (lately some trees have had a problem with the root graft)
Red Sunset	50'	rapid	3	persistent red foliage; pendulous leaves; broad upright shape

THE ASHES
Fraxinus americana, White ash

Name	Height	Rate	Zone	Notes
Autumn Purple	65'	fast	3	good street tree; reliable; tough purple fall color; seedless
Rosehill	70'	fast	3	bronze fall color; seedless, oval shape

Fraxinus pennsylvanica, Green ash

Name	Height	Rate	Zone	Notes
Marshall's Seedless	55'	fast	3	good tree; reliable; tough drought-tolerant; yellow fall color
Summit	60'	moderate	3	more upright; narrow crown; less vigorous than Marshall

THORNLESS HONEY LOCUSTS
Gleditsia triacanthos inermis

all have feathery foliage, irregular-shaped branches

Name	Height	Rate	Zone	Notes
Shademaster	60'	fast	4	upright shape; irregular
Sunburst	35'	fast	4	new foliage; bright yellow
Imperial (Lo-Gro)	40'	fast	4	spreading; round shape
Skyline	55'	fast	4	neat pyramidal crown; upright

PLANE TREE
Platanus acerifolia, London plane

Name	Height	Rate	Zone	Notes
Bloodgood	100'	fast	5	large, broad tree; not for small streets only anthracnose fungus-resistant strain

	Size	Rate of Growth	Zone	Description
FRUITLESS PEARS *Pyrus calleryana,* Callery pear				
Bradford	40'	moderate	5	excellent street tree; holds leaves late; pollution-resistant
Aristocrat	40'	moderate	5	beautiful oval shape; glossy leaves; fall color
Chanticleer	40'	moderate	5	improved fall color and leaf shape narrower
Fauriei	15'	slow	5	dwarf; round head
PIN OAK *Quercus palustris,* pin oak				
Sovereign	75'	moderate	4	only oak that moves well; subject to chlorosis; nice tree only pin oak with upright branches, others are pendulous
SOPHORA *Sophora japonica,* Sophora				
Regent	75'	moderate	4	beautiful; useful tree wide branches; small flowers
THE LINDENS *Tilia cordata,* Little leaf linden				
Greenspire	40'	moderate	3	easy to move; attractive; excellent tree; reliable
Chancellor	40'	moderate	3	excellent street tree; perfect, pyramidal shape narrower; pyramidal shape
Rancho	40'	moderate	3	even narrower; upright shape
ZELKOVA *Zelkova serrata* Village Green	90'	moderate	5	graceful; elm-like leaf; spreading; reliable train to a high head

OTHER TREES FOR DIFFICULT CITY SITUATIONS	Size	Rate of Growth	Zone	Description
Acer pseudoplatanus Sycamore maple	90'	moderate	5–9	withstands salt and wind
Ailanthus altissima Tree of Heaven	60'	fast	4–10	grows anywhere; female tree only; coarse texture; from *A Tree Grows in Brooklyn*
Albizia julibrisson rosea Silk tree	40'	fast	5–10	pink flowers; dainty leaf; spreading shape
Cedrela sinensis Chinese toon	70'	fast	5–10	looks like ailanthus; reliable
Crataegus phaenopyrum and other varieties Washington hawthorne	30'	moderate	4–7	flowers; berries
Elaeagnus angustifolia Russian olive	20'	fast	2–10	silver leaves; reliable; shrub-like
Koelreuteria paniculata Golden rain tree	35'	moderate	5–10	yellow flowers; irregular shape; hard to transplant
Magnolia soulangiana Saucer magnolia	25'	moderate	5–8	beautiful bloom; hard to transplant
Magnolia grandiflora Southern magnolia	90'	moderate	7–9	*evergreen; large flowers
Malus species Crabapple	10–30'	moderate	2–8	beautiful flowers; fruit; reliable
Phellodendron amurense Amur cork	35'	fast	3–6	low branches; disease-free

*Evergreen

OTHER TREES FOR DIFFICULT CITY SITUATIONS

	Size	Rate of Growth	Zone	Description
Quercus varieties				hard to transplant; slow-starting, but finally good; subject to insect attacks
Quercus borealis Red oak	75'	slow—moderate	3–8	good fall color
Quercus coccinea Scarlet oak	75'	slow—moderate	4–8	good fall color
Quercus phellos Willow oak	75'	moderate	5–9	fine-textured leaves; easier to transplant

Plant List 7

TREES THAT ARE HARD TO MOVE

Trees that are difficult to transplant, and/or have deep tap roots. Move only in spring. Keep well watered the first year.

Arbutus menziesii, Madrone
Betulus species, Birch
Caprinus species, Hornbeam
Carya species, Hornbeam
Crataegus species, Hawthorne
Fagus species, Beech
Gingko species, Gingko; slow-starting
Julgans species, Walnut; very slow-starting
Kalopanix pictus, Castor-aralia
Koelreuteria paniculata, Golden rain tree
Lagerstroemia indica, Crape-myrtle

Liquidambar styraciflua, Sweet gum
Lirodendron tulipfera, Tulip tree
Magnolia species, Magnolia
Nyassa sylvatica, Tupelo
Prunus species, Cherry
Pyrus species, Pear; slow-starting, except Callery pear
Quercus species, Oak, especially white and black oak
Sophora japonica, Sophora
Stewartia species, Stewartia
Ulmus species, Elm
Zelkova species, Zelkova
*Very sensitive

*Evergreen

Plant List 8

COMMONLY USED DECIDUOUS SHRUBS

Different varieties of each species grow to different heights at maturity. Check the mature height of the variety sold by your nursery.

	Size	Rate of Growth	Zone	Description
Berberis varieties Barberry	3–10'	fast	3–10	reliable; tough, thorny; vigorous habit; berries; fall color
Chaenomeles varieties Flowering quince	3–6'	moderate	4–9	early flowers; many bright colors; watch for scale
Cornus stolinifera Red osier dogwood	7'	fast	2–9	red or yellow stems in winter; very invasive though, spreads
Cotoneaster varieties Cotoneaster	1–16'	moderate	3–10	very useful; sun; attractive leaves; berries; fall color
Cytisus species Broom	1–9'	slow	5–10	sun; dry soil; yellow flowers; interesting winter shape
Euonymus alata Burning bush, Winged euonymus	9'	fast	3–10	spectacular fall color; berries; reliable; sun; city-tolerant
Forsythia varieties Forsythia	9'	fast	5–8	early yellow flowers; good screen plant; vigorous; tough; city-tolerant
Fothergilla varieties Large fothergilla	9'	fast	5–9	early, fuzzy flowers; upright shape; good fall color
Hibiscus rosa-sinensis Hibiscus, many colors	30'	fast	9–10	most useful shrub; flowers daily; shears well

	Size	Rate of Growth	Zone	Description
Hibiscus syriacus Althea, Rose of Sharon	15'	moderate	5–10	summer-blooming
Hydrangea varieties Hydrangea	3–20'	fast	4–10	big flowers; coarse leaves; easy to grow anywhere; some varieties very beautiful
Pyracantha coccinea lalandi Firethorn	8'	moderate	6–9	beautiful berries; small flowers; needs support; flowers on three-year wood
Rosa varieties Rose	3–10'	fast	3–9	beautiful flowers; sun; good soil; high maintenance, except for old fashioned bush varieties
Viburnum varieties Viburnam, many common names	5–15'	fast	5–9	good flowers; very useful shrubs; good foliage

DECIDUOUS SHRUBS FOR USE WHERE MORE CHOICE VARIETIES WILL NOT GROW

These shrubs are very vigorous and will grow almost anywhere. They are not as ornamental as the shrubs listed above.

	Size	Rate of Growth	Zone	Description
Ligustrum varieties Privet	to 30'	fast	3–9	planted too often for hedges, where low growth is wanted; useful for tall screen
Lonicera varieties Bush honeysuckle	6–15'	fast	2–8	reliable flowers; berries; round shape

	Size	Rate of Growth	Zone	Description
Philadelphius coronarius Mock-orange	9'	fast	4–9	white fragrant flowers; tough; old-fashioned favorite
Potentilla fruticosa Bush cinquefoil	4'	fast	2–9	yellow flowers; reliable; dry soil; useful plant for low care; exposed situations
Spirea varieties Bridal wreath, Spirea	1–10'	fast	4–9	charming flowers; twiggy bush; many varieties available
Syringea varieties Lilac	6–20'	fast	3–9	beautiful flowers; uninteresting for 50 weeks of the year; reliable; city-tolerant; like lime; French hybrid lilacs are better ornamentals with better blooms and smaller bushes, but are less reliable
Vaccinium varieties Blueberry	3–12'	moderate	3–7	edible fruit; good fall color; attractive when pruned; acid soil

Plant List 9

BEST COMMONLY USED EVERGREEN SHRUBS

Different varieties of each species grow to different heights at maturity. Check the mature height of the variety sold in your nursery.

	Size	Rate of Growth	Zone	Description
Albelia grandiflora Albelia	3–6'	moderate	6–10	neat; drought-resistant; blooms all summer
Arbutus unedo Strawberry tree	10–30'	slow	8–10	acid soil; attractive flowers, fruit, and bark

	Size	Rate of Growth	Zone	Description
Azalea varieties Azalea, many kinds	3–10'	slow	5–9	acid; peaty soil; beautiful flowers; part shade
Buxus varieties Common box	4–20'	slow	5–10	splendid green shrub; shears well; shade; formal
Camellia japonica Camellia	4–30'	slow	7–10	beautiful flowers; acid soil; partial shade
Daphne varieties Daphne	1½–6'	slow	4–8	temperamental; pink flowers; fragrant; charming shrub
Ilex varieties Holly	2–25'	slow	5–9	attractive shiny foliage; berries; many varieties need acid soil and shade
Juniperus varieties Low-spreading juniper	1–10'	moderate	2–10	feathery foliage; many shapes; sun
Kalmia latifolia Mountain laurel	20'	slow	5–9	good foliage; flowers; acid soil; shade
Leucothoe catesbaei Drooping leucothos	5'	moderate	4–9	graceful mound of green; shade; acid soil
Nandia domestica Heavenly bamboo	8'	moderate	7–10	flowers; colored foliage; long-lasting fruit
Nerium orleander Orleander	20'	fast	8–10	good flowers; reliable; sun
Pieris varieties Andromeda	4–12'	moderate	4–9	very attractive foliage; flowers; shade; acid soil

	Size	Rate of Growth	Zone	Description
Pinus mugo mughus Mugo pine	3–6'	moderate	2–9	attractive; dramatic foliage; full sun; tough
Pittosporum tobira Pittosporum, Japanese	10'	fast	8–10	attractive foliage; fragrant flowers; stands dry soil
Rhododendron varieties Rhododendron, many kinds	3–20'	slow	4–9	most beautiful shrubs; flowers impressive; shade; acid soil buy in bloom for best color
Rhododendron, Southern varieties			7–9	less hardy
Taxus varieties Yew	1–30'	moderate	5–8	best foliage for winter; reliable; shade; no lime; shears well
Podocarpus	to 80' shear to keep small	moderate	9–10	use Podocarpus for similar foliage effect as yew

Plant List 10

BEST LOW-GROWING SHRUBS FOR FOUNDATION PLANTING

EVERGREEN	Size	Rate of Growth	Zone	Description
Azalea obtusum and *kaempferi* hybrids *Kurume,* named azaleas	3'	slow	6–9 5–9 5–9	shade; acid soil; pick in bloom for best color; *kaempferi* varieties stand more shade; semi-evergreen
Buxus microphylla koreana Korean box	2'	slow	5–10	neat mound; shade

	Size	Rate of Growth	Zone	Description
Daphne cneorum Rose daphne	1½'	slow	4–8	fragrant pink flowers; temperamental
Erica carnea Spring heath	1'	slow	5–7	sandy; acid soil; sun; neat choice plant; pink flowers
Gardenia jasminoides Cape jasmine	5'	slow	8–9	beautiful; fragrant flowers; good foliage; shade; moisture; acid soil
Ilex crenata convexa Japanese holly	6'	slow	5–9	neat; glossy foliage; shears well; acid soil; semishade
Ilex helleri Heller holly	2'	slow	5–9	lovely green mound; acid soil; shade
Ilex vomitoria nana Dwarf yaupon	2'	moderate	8–10	stands heat; dry soil; reliable; gray-green
Juniperus chinensis pfitzerana compacta Compact pfitzer juniper	3'	moderate	3–10	feathery foliage; very useful; sun
Juniperus chinensis sargentii Sargent juniper	1'	moderate	4–10	creeping; attractive; sun
Juniperus horizontalis plumosa Andorra juniper	1'	moderate	2–9	sun attractive mound; purple in winter
Juniperus horizontalis wiltoni Blue rug juniper	1'	moderate	3–10	sun; attractive; creeping; vigorous; drapes over walls and rocks; blue color
Leucothoe catesbaei Drooping leucothoe	5'	moderate	4–9	graceful green mound; acid soil; shade

Plant				
Mahonia aquifolium Oregon grape holly	3'	slow	5–10	dry sandy soil, shade; good foliage; spreads
Pieris floribunda Mountain andromeda	3'	moderate	5–8	attractive; graceful; acid soil; shade
Pinus mugo mughus Mugo pine	6'	moderate	2–9	crisp foliage; sun; well-drained soil
Pittosporum tobira Wheeler's dwarf Wheeler's dwarf pittosporum	3'	moderate	8–10	attractive foliage; fragrant blooms; stands dry soil
Rhododendron laetivirens wilsonii Wilson rhododendron	3'	slow	5–9	pink bloom; small leaf; stands deep shade
Rhododendron PJM PJM rhododendron (Weston Nurseries, Mass.)	5'	moderate	5–8	blooms very early; purple or pink; stands sun and cold; vigorous
Rhododendron catawbiense compactum Catawbiense low-growing hybrids	3'	slow	5–9	semishade; some sun; big blooms; choose in bloom for best colors; nonhybrids grow 12' tall
Lees Dark Purple	4'	slow	5–9	purple
Boule de Neige	6'	slow	5–9	best white flowers; semishade, reliable
Nova zembla	6'	slow	5–9	red
Cunningham's White	4'	slow	5–9	white
Chionoides	4'	slow	5–9	white with yellow
Taxus baccata repandens Spreading English yew	2'	slow	4–8	low-spreading; semishade; no lime; best winter color; useful shrub
Taxus media densiformis Spreading yew densiform	5'	slow	4–8	bushy; vigorous; most useful; no lime; good winter color; shears well
Taxus media Hicksii Hicks Yew	8'	slow	4–8	upright; good accent plant; shears well; good winter color; berries; makes a good screen

	Size	Rate of Growth	Zone	Description
Thuja occidentalis globosa Globe arborvitae	4'	slow	3–9	holds round, globe-like shape; bright green
Yucca filamentosa Adams needle	3'	moderate	4–10	sun; dry conditions; stiff, pointed leaves; 3' flower spike
DECIDUOUS	Size	Rate of Growth	Zone	Description
Azaleas mollis varieties	5'	slow	5–9	yellow; orange blooms; bloom late; acid soil; sun or semishade
Exbury hybrids, all others	3–6'	slow	5–9	magnificent colors—yellow, orange, white, brown, pink, red; acid soil; semishade; choose in bloom
Berberis thunbergii atropurpurae nana Crimson pigmy barberry	2'	fast	4–9	neat shrub; red leaves; thorns; sun
Cotoneaster microphylla Small-leafed cotoneaster	3'	slow	4–10	sun; neat, small leaves; semi-evergreen; good fruit
Fothergilla gardeni Dwarf fothergilla	3'	moderate	5–9	nice; early bloom; sun; good fall color
Viburnum carlesii Fragrant viburnum carlesii	5'	slow	5–9	lovely; fragrant flowers; round shrubs

Plant List 11

Good for understory planting.

SHRUBS THAT GROW IN THE SHADE

	Size	Rate of Growth	Hardy to Zone	Description
Albelia grandiflora Glossy albelia	6'	fast	5	good foliage; small flowers
Acanthopanaxa sieb oldianus Acanthopanax	9'	fast	4	good foliage; grows in city
Aronia arbutofolia Choke cherry	10'	fast	4	dependable; open shape
Azalea kaempferi Torch azalea	12'	moderate	5	beautiful red-orange flowers; withstands full shade; acid soil
Azalea varieties Azalea	3–15'	moderate	5	semishade for best bloom; acid soil
Berberis thunbergi Japanese barberry	7'	fast	5	thorns; dependable; does not carry wheat rust disease
Buxus sempervirens Common box	20'	slow	6	*evergreen; shears well
Calycanthus floridus Carolina all spice	9'	moderate	4	any soil; fragrant flowers; aromatic leaves
Camellia japonica Camellia	40'	slow	7	*evergreen; beautiful blooms; acid soil

* Evergreen.

	Size	Rate of Growth	Hardy to Zone	Description
Clethra alnifolia Summersweet	9'	fast	3	fragrant bloom; moist soil
Daphne mezereum February daphne	3'	slow	4	flowers; hard to grow; very fragrant
Ilex varieties Holly	3–30'	slow	3–6	*evergreen; attractive; many kinds; acid soil
Hydrangea arborescens Hills of Snow	3'	fast	4	big; white flowers
Hamemelis varieties Chinese witch hazel Vernal witch hazel	10–30'	fast	5 4	big bushes; yellow, fragrant flowers fall blooming blooms in February
Kalmia latifolia Mountain laurel	15'	slow	5	*evergreen; flowers; attractive foliage; acid soil
Leucothoe catesbaei Drooping leucothoe	6'	moderate	6	*evergreen; graceful
Mahonia aquifolium Oregon holly-grape	3'	moderate	5	*semi-evergreen; excellent plant; dry, sandy soil
Myrica pennsylvanica Bayberry	6'	moderate	2	*semi-evergreen; aromatic berries; sexes separate; sandy soil
Pieris varieties Andromeda	3–6'	moderate	4–7	*evergreen; tolerates heavy shade; acid soil
Rhamnus, frangula Alder, buckthorn	12'	fast	2	any soil; berries

	Size		Zone	Description
Rhododendron maximum Rosebay rhododendron	35'	moderate	4	*evergreen; stands heavy shade; good blooms; good foliage which curls at 32° F.
Rhododendron varieties Rhododendron	3–15'	moderate	5–7	*evergreen; variety of flower colors and shapes; acid soil
Symphoricarpos species Snowberry, Coralberry	3–6'	moderate	2	dull shrubs; reliable; nice berries
Taxus varieties Yew	3–50'	slow	4–7	*evergreen; attractive foliage; good green winter color
Vaccinium corymbosum Blueberry	12'	moderate	3	good fall color; edible fruit; acid soil
Viburnum sieboldi Siebold viburnum	30'	moderate	4	attractive foliage; flowers; fruit; useful; vigorous

Plant List 12

BEST GROUND COVERS FOR SUN

	Size	Planting distance, spacing	Zone	Description
EVERGREEN				
Ameria maritima Thrift	6"	8" apart	5–9	sandy soil; pink flowers
Arctostaphylos uva-ursi Bearberry	6"	2'	2–9	sandy; acid soil; red berries; hard to transplant; also grows in semishade

EVERGREEN	Size	Planting distance, spacing	Zone	Description
Cotoneaster apiculata Cranberry cotoneaster	3'	3'	4–10	semi-evergreen; red berries; well-drained soil; pink flowers
Cotoneaster adpressa praecox Early cotoneaster	18"	3'	5–10	semi-evergreen; red berries; partial shade in South
Erica carnea Spring heath	1'	12"	5–7	sandy; acid soil; neat; rosy blooms
Euonymus fortunei radicans Wintercreeper	1'	18"	5–9	attractive foliage; informal in appearance unless sheared; spreads; climbs; very useful; sun or shade
Euonymus fortunei colorata	1'	18"	5–9	same as above but has red-bronze leaves all winter
Gazenia rigens African daisy	9"	9"	9–10	charming flowers; well-drained soil
Ice plant Many Latin names	12"	8"	10	flowers during day; succulent; sandy soil; spreads; useful for sunny sea coast
Juniperus low-grading varieties				most maintenance free; neat ground cover for sun; well-drained soil
Juniperus chinensis sargentii Sargent juniper	1'	2'	4–10	green; creeping
Juniperus horizontalis plumosa Andorra juniper	1'	2'	2–9	purple in winter; low mound
Juniperus horizontalis wiltoni Blue rug juniper	1'	2'	3–10	blue color; creeping

	Size	Planting distance, spacing	Zone	Description
Juniperus chinensis pfitzerans compacta Compact Pfitzer juniper	3'	3'	3–10	blue-green color; high enough to hide weeds
Juniperus chinensis pfitzerana Pfitzer juniper	5'	4'	2–10	gray-green; more vigorous
Juniperus chinensis hetzi glauca Hetz blue juniper	6'	5'	4–10	blue-green; very vigorous and spreading
Phlox sublata Moss pink, Ground phlox	6"	12"	4–10	creeping; mass of spring bloom; well-drained soil
DECIDUOUS				
Cerastium tomentosum Snow-in-Summer	6"	12" apart	4–10	silvery leaves; white flowers; spreads rapidly; crowds less vigorous flowers
Coronilla varia Crown vetch	24"	2'	3–9	pink flowers; good for steep banks; doesn't like acid soil
Cotoneaster horizontalis Rock cotoneaster	3'	4'	5–10	good fall color; berries; pink flowers; well-drained soil; semishade in South
Cytisus praecox Warminster broom	6'	3'	5–10	upright shrubs; dry sandy soil; early yellow blooms; green twigs in winter
Cytisus hybrids, Broom 'California,' 'Pomona,' 'San Francisco,' 'Stanford'	3–6'	3'	7–10	beautiful colors; very good in California; upright
Cytisus nigricans Spike broom	3'	3'	5–10	most reliable; yellow flowers; dry black pods; upright; informal appearance

DECIDUOUS	Size	Planting distance, spacing	Zone	Description
Dicksonia punctilobula Hay-scented fern	15"	12"	6–9	spreads; tough; feathery; sun or shade
Sedum acre, spurium and others Stone crop, Sedum	4"	8"	4–10	semi-evergreen succulents; dense, low mats of foliage; blooms; useful plants; well-drained soil
Thymus serpyllum Creeping thyme	4"	8"	5–10	flowers; scented foliage; well-drained soil; attractive mat of foliage; tiny leaves

Plant List 13

BEST GROUND COVERS FOR SHADE

EVERGREEN	Size	Planting distance, spacing	Zone	Description
Ajuga reptans Bugle weed	4"	8" apart	5–9	purple flowers; spreads well
Asarum europaeum Wild ginger	5"	8"	5–8	glossy, round leaves; woodland soil
Hedera helix baltica Baltic ivy	8"	12"	5–9	very neat; attractive foliage; reliable; spreads; formal appearance; no lime
Ophiopogon japonicus Mondo grass	8"	9"	7–10	attractive; grasslike foliage; clumps of green; spreads; lilac flower; sun or shade

Pachysandra terminalis Japanese spurge	6"	9"	5–8	very neat; attractive; reliable; good soil; spreads vigorously
Vinca minor periwinkle	6"	9"	5–10	most attractive leaf; dainty; graceful; spreads; blue flower; well-drained, good soil

DECIDUOUS

Convallaria major Lily-of-the-valley	10"	12"	4–9	tough; reliable; spreads slowly; most fragrant bloom
Hemerocallis Day lily	3'	18"	3–10	reliable; summer flowers; sun or shade
Hosta varieties Plantain lily, Funkia	18"	12"	4–10	tough; reliable; good soil; will grow under trees where few things will survive; tall summer blooms

Plant List 14

FAST-GROWING VINES FOR TRELLISES AND FENCES

NOTE: All vigorous vines *MUST* be pruned back each spring or they get out of control and become pests.

	Hardy to Zone	Growth in one year	Description
Actinidia arguta Bower actinidia	4	15–20'	twining

	Hardy to Zone	Growth in one year		Description
Actinidia chinensis *Chinese actinidia	7	25'	twining	vigorous; will cover 30 x 30 square feet
Bignonia capreolata Cross vine	6	15'	tendrils	semi-evergreen; flowers
Campensis grandiflora Chinese trumpet vine	7	5–10'	tendrils	dry soil;
Campenis radicans "Mme. Galens" Trumpet vine	4	10'	tendrils	Both: big flowers; coarse leaves; need tying for support
Clematis paniculata Sweet autumn clematis	5	15'	twining	fragrant flowers; vigorous; *one of the best*
Clematis vitabella Traveller's joy	4	20'	twining	fragrant flowers; vigorous
Lonicera japonica *Fragrant honeysuckle	4	20'	twining	can become a pest if out of control; roots where it touches ground
Lonicera Tellmaniana Tellmann honeysuckle	6	10'	twining	needs cool roots; better flowers
Lonicera sempervirens Trumpet honeysuckle	4	10'	twining	big flowers; dry soil; gets aphids
Passiflora species Passion flowers	7	6–15'	tendrils	fruits edible; flowers; not dense
Pueraria Thumbergiana *Kudzu vine	6	30–50'	twining	fastest grower; can get 75'; coarse leaves; dry soil

Vitis coignetiae *Glory vine	5	40'	tendrils	very rapid grower
Vitis labrusca "Concord" Concord grape	3	20'	tendrils	good fruit
Wisteria species *Wisteria	4–5	7'	twining	should be grown on metal pipes—will break wood, gutters, drainpipes; flowers

Plant List 15

EVERGREEN VINES FOR THE SOUTH

For use to provide year-round shade.

	Zone	Growth in one year		Description
Boussingaultia basselloides *Madeira vine	9–10	4–20'	tendrils	can get out of control
Cobaea scandens Cup and saucer vine	9–10	6—10'	tendrils	vigorous; can grow to 40' long
Doxantha unguis-cati *Cat-claw vine	8–10	20'	tendrils with thorns	clings to hot stone or wood
Euonymus fortunei species Winter creeper	5–9	5'	clinging	
Ficus pumila Creeping fig	9–10	7'	clinging	figs inedible

* Vines that *must* be controlled.

	Zone	Growth in one year	Description
Hedera canariensis Algerian ivy	7–10	clinging	
Smilaw megalantha Coral greenbriar	7–10	twining	needs male and female plants for fruit

WINDBREAK PLANTS FOR WIND CONTROL AND SHELTER BELTS

Shelterbelts should be broadside to the winter wind and long enough to give good protection. Deciduous material grows fastest. For best protection, there should be two or three rows, staggered. One should be tall, fast-growing, deciduous material; the second, evergreen; the third shrubs and small trees. If small trees are planted inside the shelter belt, protected by the other two, it can be choice flowering material from other lists.

Most of the trees recommended here are not suitable near buildings, and should be between 20 and 60 feet from them. The closer the trees are to the buildings however, the more effective they will be. The trees recommended here will grow quickly, withstand cold, heat, drought and wind. Many are soft-wooded and may lose branches in storms. In general, the faster a tree grows, the more likely it will be to have soft wood which can break easily in storms. On the Great Plains, where conditions are harsh, shelterbelts give wind protection, privacy, and relief from the boundless open space of the prairies.

Spacing. For effective windbreaks, close spacing is necessary. It may be two, four, or six feet, depending on the species. The aim is a wall of leaves or needles. All plants can be thickened by correct shearing. Closely spaced plants compete for water and nutrients. Their availability limits growth. If the soil is improved at planting time with peat moss, old manure, and fertilizer, the growth rate will be more satisfactory.

Plant List 16

WINDBREAK PLANTS FOR THE GREAT PLAINS

Useful for wind control and shelter belts.

	Size	Spacing	Growth Rate	Zone	Description
Acer ginnala Amur maple	20'	4' apart	slow	2–9	no care, good fall color
Acer negundo Box-elder	60'	6'	fast	2–9	weak-wooded but reliable; can be removed when better trees grow
Amelanchier alnifolia Saskatoon	20'	4'	moderate	2–7	good shrub; edible berries; spreads by suckers (gets fire blight and cedar-apple rust)
Caragana arborescens Siberian pea tree	18'	4'	moderate	2–7	very hard shrub; drought-resistant
Eleagnus angustifolia Russian olive	20'	6'	fast	2–10	silvery leaves; reliable
Fraxinus pennsylvanica Green ash	60'	6'	fast	2–9	good shade tree
Juniperus communis Common juniper	3–30'	2'	moderate	2–6	*evergreen; buy the upright-growing variety
Lonerica tatarica Tatarian honeysuckle	9'	3'	fast	3–6	dependable; little flowers
Maclura pomifera Osage-orange	60'	6'	fast	5–9	very spreading; thorns; rough

*Evergreen

	Size	Spacing	Growth Rate	Zone	Description
Picea glauca White spruce	90'	6'	slow	2–5	*evergreen; best evergreen for wind screen
Picea pungens Colorado blue spruce	100'	6'	moderate	2–6	*evergreen; best evergreen for wind screen; blue color
Pinus banksiana Jack pine	75'	4'	moderate	2–8	*evergreen; dry soil; useful where others fail
Pinus sylvestris Scotch pine	70'	6'	moderate	2–7	*evergreen; good, wide
Populus varieties Poplar, cottonwood	50–100'	4'	fastest	2–9	most versatile; useful tree
Prunus virginiana Choke cherry	30'	4'	fast	2–9	birds like the fruit
Quercus macrocarpa Bur oak	75'	12'	slow	2–9	broad, hardy tree
Salix alba White willow, upright	75'	6'	fast	2–7	prefers moist soil
Shepherdia argentea Buffalo berry	18'	3'	moderate	2–7	shrub; tolerant of alkaline soil; likes cool roots
Ulmus pumila Dwarf elm	75'	6'	fast	2–8	less susceptible to Dutch elm disease

Plant List 17

WINDBREAK PLANTS FOR NORMAL SOILS

Note: All the plants listed under WINDBREAKS FOR THE GREAT PLAINS, List # 16, may also be used.

	Size	Spacing	Growth Rate	Zone	Description
Acer species Maple species	25–90'	4' apart	moderate	2–9	good trees
Carpinus betulus European hornbeam	60'	4'	slow	5–9	neat, attractive tree; shears well
Cornus mas Cronelian cherry	24'	4'	moderate	4–8	pest-free; attractive; small flowers; fruit
Crataegus phaenopyrum Washington hawthorne	30'	4'	moderate	4–7	flowers; berries
Eucalyptus species Red, white, or silver dollar gum	100'+	6'	fastest	9–10	big trees; effective; not near buildings
Forsythia intermidia Border forsythia	9'	4'	fast	4–8	flowers; withstands some shade
Ligustrum amurense Amur privet	15'	2'	fast	3–6	shears well; do not use common privet
Ligustrum japonicum Japanese privet	6–18'	3'	fast	7–9	*evergreen; useful; stands shade
Philadelphus coronaris Sweet mock-orange	9'	3'	fast	4–9	fragrant flowers; stands dry soil; stands some shade
Picea abies Norway spruce	100'	6'	fast	2–6	*excellent evergreen

*Evergreen

	Size	Spacing	Growth Rate	Zone	Description
Pinus nigra Austrian pine	90'	6'	moderate	4–7	*evergreen; stands alkaline soil, city conditions
Pinus strobus White pine	100'	6'	fast	3–7	*evergreen; moist, sandy soil; beautiful tree
Quercus imbricaria Shingle oak	75'	12'	slow	5–8	holds some dry leaves in winter; shears well
Rhamnus frangula columnaris Tall hedge buckthorn	12'	2'	fast	2–8	narrow; upright; vigorous shrub; makes a tight hedge with little shearing; stays 12' high
Syringa amurensis Japanese lilac tree	30'	4'	fast	4–7	good flowers; attractive
Syringa vulgaris Common lilac	20'	2'	fast	3–7	hardy; reliable; fragrant blooms
Tilia cordata "Greenspire" Greenspire little leaf linden	40'	4'	moderate	3–7	good shape; nice foliage; upright; buy low-branched specimens for windbreaks
Viburnum prunifolium Blackhaw	15'	3'	fast	3–7	flowers; berries
Viburnum sieboldi Siebold viburnum	30'	4'	fast	4–8	vigorous; attractive; modest flowers; berries

Plant List 18

DROUGHT-RESISTANT PLANTS

Plants for the Southwest Desert. Alkaline soil resistant.   **Hardy to Zone**

Agave	7
Boojam tree	7
Brittlebush	7
Cacti	6
Catclaw (acacia)	7
Creosote bush	7
Hackberry, spiny	6
Jojoba	7
Mesquite	6
Ocotillo	7
Paloverde	7
Sotol	7
Tesota	7
Yucca	5

Plants for Areas with Less Than 10″ of Rainfall.
Alkaline soil resistant.   **Hardy to Zone**

One-seed juniper	4
Rocky mountain juniper	3
Apache plume	4
Bitterbush, Antelope	4
Desert willow	6
Fontanesia, Fortune	6
Forestiera, New Mexican	4
Golden rain tree	5
Leadplant	4
Rabbitbrush	3
Sagebrush	4
Saltbrush	4
Tamarix, Athel	8

Drought-Resistant Plants. Withstand dry soil.   **Hardy to Zone**

TREES—NEEDLED EVERGREENS	
Arborvitae, eastern, oriental	4*
Cypress, Arizona, Monterey	7*
Casaurina species (beefwood)	10
Fir, white	4*
Juniper species	3*
Pine, jack, scotch, mugo	2*
ponderosa, bristlecone (slow-growing)	5*
scrub, pitch, Austrian	4*
torrey, canary	8
Spruce, Colorado, Englemann	3*
black hills	4

Drought-Resistant Plants. Withstand dry soil.	**Hardy to Zone**
TREES—BROADLEAFED	
Acacia, gossamer Sydney	10
Ailanthus (tree of heaven)	4
Albizia, silk tree (mimosa)	6*
Angelica tree (aralia)	2
Ash, green, European mountain	4*
velvet	7
Australian tea tree	9
Bauhinia	10
Birch, cutleaf weeping	4*
grey	5
Box-elder	2
Bottle-tree (brachychiton)	10
Buckeye	4*
Carob	10
Chinaberry (melia)	7
Cottonwood	3*
Crabapple, flowering	3*
Elm, Siberian (stands alkaline soil)	2*
most resistant to Dutch elm disease	
Eucalyptus	9
Fig (*ficus* species)	6–10
Golden rain tree	5*
Grevillea	10
Hackberry	3*
Honey locust, thornless	4*
Jerusalem thorn (parkinsonia)	9
Jujube	5*
Linden	4
Locust, black	5*
Maple, amur, silver	3*
Manchurian, tatarian	4*
Norway	4
Melaleuca (cajeput)	10
Mesquite	8*
Mulberry	6*
Oak, California black, live	7*
chestnut	4*
pin	4
red	3
burr	2*
Olive	9*
Osage orange (maclura)	5
Pecan	6
Pepper tree (schinus)	9*
Poplar, white	3
Redbud, eastern	5
Russian olive (tolerates alkaline soil)	3*

Drought-Resistant Plants. Withstand dry soil.	**Hardy to Zone**
TREES—BROADLEAFED (cont.)	
Sophora	4
Sycamore	5*
Walnut, black	4*
SHRUBS	
Almond, Russian, prairie	3*
Autumn sage	7
Beauty bush	7*
Barberry, Japanese, Mentor	5
Broom (Acid soil)	6
Bayberry (Acid Soil)	2
Bottlebrush, lemon	9
Buckthorn, common, rock, Duhurian	2*
Buffalo-berry, Canada russet	2*
(stands alkaline soil)	
Butcher's broom (ruscus)	7
Butterfly bush, fountain	5*
Ceanothus, inland	4**
Chaste-tree, cut-leafed	5*
Cherry, western, sand	3
Dogwood, Siberian	3*
gray	4
Elderberry, blueberry	5*
Euphorbia, milkbush	10**
Firethorn, laland	5*
Forsythia	5*
Greasewood	4*
Hawthorne, cockspur, downey, English	4*
Hebe, species	7
Honeysuckle, tatarian, Zabel	3*
amur	4*
winter	5*
Lilac, late (villosa)	2*
common	3*
Japanese tree	4*
Persian	5*
Mock-orange, virginal, sweet	5*
Mountain mahogany	4**
Ninebark	2
Oleander	7
Peach, pigmy, globe Russian, Siberian	5*
Pea shrub (pea tree), Siberian, maximowicz	2*
little leaf, pygmaea	3*
Pittosporum	8
Plum, flowering, Newport, beach	3*
Privet	3*
Quince, flowering, Japanese	5*
Rose, Austrian copper, Harrison's yellow	3*

Drought-Resistant Plants. Withstand dry soil.   **Hardy to Zone**

SHRUBS (cont.)	
Rosemary	6
Rosewood, Arizona	6**
Serviceberry, shadblow, saskatoon	3*
Smoke tree	5*
Snowberry	4**
Sophora, vetch	5
Spirea, Nippon, Vanhoutte	4*
Sumac	2*
Tamarix, five stamen	2
parvifolio, Odessa	4*
kasgar	6**
Viburnum, nannyberry, cranberry bush	2*
Manchurian	2*
snowball	4
Wayfaring tree (*lantana rugosum*)	3*
Yucca	4**

* 10"–20" Rainfall
** Less than 10" rainfall

Plant List 19

SEQUENCE OF BLOOM

Indicated blooming dates are the approximate ones for Plant Hardiness Zone 5. For more northerly areas, add about one week per zone; subtract for more southerly zones.

	Apr.	May	June	July	Aug.
Andromeda (*Pieris japonica, P. floribunda*), white	■				
*Shadblow, Serviceberry (*Amalanchier canadensis*), white		■			
*Star magnolia (*Magnolia stellata*), white		■			
Forsythia (*Forsythia* species)		■			
Korean azalea (*Rhododendron macronultaum*)		■			
*Saucer magnolia (*Magnolia soulangeana*), white, pink		■			
*Weeping cherry (*Prunus subhirtella*), pink		■			
*Beach plum (*Prunus maritami*), white		■			
Quince (*Chaenomeles lagenaria*), orange, pink, white		■			
*Crabapple (*Malus species*), white, pink		■			
*Dogwood (*Carnus florida*), white, pink		■			
*Kwansan cherry (*Prunus serrulata "Kwansan"*), pink		■			
*English hawthorne (*Crataegus oxycantha*), pink, white		■			
*Redbud (*Circus canadensis*), pink		■			

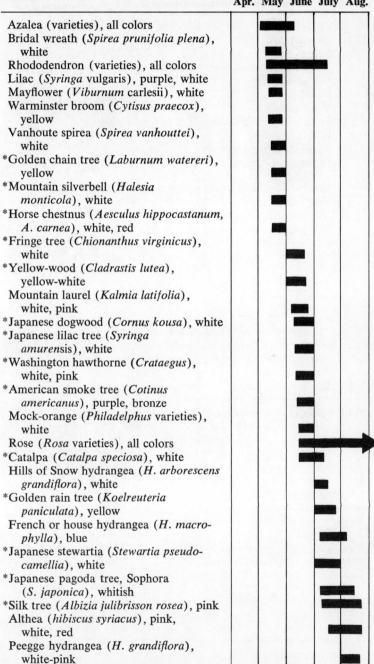

	Apr.	May	June	July	Aug.

Azalea (varieties), all colors

Bridal wreath (*Spirea prunifolia plena*),
   white

Rhododendron (varieties), all colors

Lilac (*Syringa* vulgaris), purple, white

Mayflower (*Viburnum* carlesii), white

Warminster broom (*Cytisus praecox*),
   yellow

Vanhoute spirea (*Spirea vanhouttei*),
   white

*Golden chain tree (*Laburnum watereri*),
   yellow

*Mountain silverbell (*Halesia
   monticola*), white

*Horse chestnus (*Aesculus hippocastanum,
   A. carnea*), white, red

*Fringe tree (*Chionanthus virginicus*),
   white

*Yellow-wood (*Cladrastis lutea*),
   yellow-white

Mountain laurel (*Kalmia latifolia*),
   white, pink

*Japanese dogwood (*Cornus kousa*), white

*Japanese lilac tree (*Syringa
   amuren*sis), white

*Washington hawthorne (*Crataegus*),
   white, pink

*American smoke tree (*Cotinus
   americanus*), purple, bronze

Mock-orange (*Philadelphus* varieties),
   white

Rose (*Rosa* varieties), all colors

*Catalpa (*Catalpa speciosa*), white

Hills of Snow hydrangea (*H. arborescens
   grandiflora*), white

*Golden rain tree (*Koelreuteria
   paniculata*), yellow

French or house hydrangea (*H. macro-
   phylla*), blue

*Japanese stewartia (*Stewartia pseudo-
   camellia*), white

*Japanese pagoda tree, Sophora
   (*S. japonica*), whitish

*Silk tree (*Albizia julibrisson rosea*), pink

Althea (*hibiscus syriacus*), pink,
   white, red

Peegge hydrangea (*H. grandiflora*),
   white-pink

* Trees

Plant List 20

GROWTH-RATE COMPARISON CHART

Height in ten years.

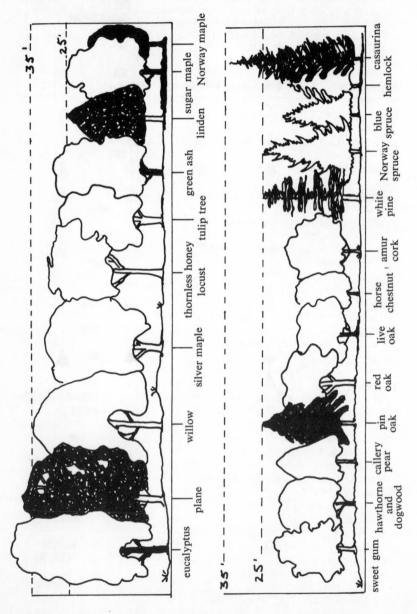

Plant List 21

POLLUTION SENSITIVITY

Pollutants inhibit growth and longevity. Susceptibility varies with each pollutant and each type of tree, even between different trees of the same kind. Tests are being done to determine sensitivity. These are some results. Salt is a problem both on winter roads and from ocean spray at the seashore.

Name of Tree	Salt	Sodium Dioxide	Ozone	Oxides of Nitrogen
White spruce	△	△	△	▲
Hemlock	▲	▲	▲	
White pine	▲	▲	▲	▲
Austrian pine	△	△	▲	▲
Japanese black pine	△			
Sugar, Red maple	▲	△	△	▲
Sycamore maple	△	△	△	
Pin oak	▲		▲	
Red oak, Black oak	△	△	△	
American linden	▲		▲	▲
Ironwood	▲	△		▲
Beech	△	▲		▲
Willow	△	▲	▲	
White dogwood		△	△	
Birch	△			
Black cherry	△			
Russian olive	△			
Sophora	△			

Pollution tolerant. △   Pollution sensitive. ▲
* Absence of symbol indicates insufficient data.

GLOSSARY

Berm. A small mound of earth, used for privacy or to block wind.

Deciduous. Plants which lose their leaves or needles and are bare in winter.

Evergreen. Plants which retain their leaves or needles all year. Most drop the old leaves after two or three years.

Erosion. Soil that washes or blows away, leaving gullies or subsoil exposed.

Heat island effect. Heat retention phenomenon of cities that makes them warmer than the surrounding suburbs, and warmer than their expected zone of hardiness.

Leeward. The side towards which the wind blows.

Landforms. Also "earthform." Refers to the shape of the land, usually a berm or hill.

Microclimate. The particular climate of a very small area.

Microenvironment. Factors affecting an area, including water, soil, wind, temperature pollution, etc., that characterize a particular location.

Mulch. Decayed plant material (i.e., leaves, grass) or other material (i.e., plastic) which covers the soil and retards evaporation of moisture.

Root-prune. Cut the roots of a tree or plant to prepare it for moving.

Site.   A particular location. Refers to the ground contours and boundaries primarily.

Starter solution.   A weak solution of soluble fertilizer used for watering at planting time.

Velocity.   Speed (of wind).

Vegetation.   Anything that grows.

Water stress.   A plant's response to drought.

Wind-shadows.   Area of dead air space or lowered wind velocity behind a windbreak.

Windward.   The side from which the wind blows.

Underplanting.   Plants used to fill spaces under a high tree canopy.

INDEX

182 *Index*